The
Buzzword
Bingo
Book

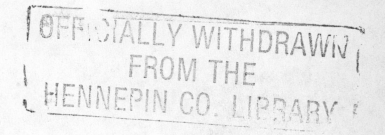

The Buzzword Bingo Book

The Complete, Definitive Guide to the Underground Workplace Game of Corporate Jargon and Doublespeak

Lara Stein and Benjamin Yoskovitz

VILLARD ▪▪▪ NEW YORK ▪▪▪ A LARK PRODUCTION

VILLARD BOOKS is a registered trademark of Random House, Inc.

Library of Congress Cataloging-in-Publication Data

Stein, Lara.
The Buzzword Bingo Book: the complete, definitive guide to the
underground workplace game of corporate jargon and doublespeak/
Lara Stein and Benjamin Yoskovitz.
p.   cm.
ISBN 0-375-75348-6
1. Management—Terminology—Humor. 2. Communication in management—Humor.
3. English language—New words—Humor. 4. Jargon (Terminology)—Humor.
I. Yoskovitz, Benjamin. II. Title. III. Title: Buzzword Bingo book.
HD30.17.S74   1999
658'.001'4—dc21   98-46220

Random House website address: www.atrandom.com
Printed in the United States of America on acid-free paper

24689753
First Edition

DESIGN BY LISA SLOANE

For the Gipper, who taught us a thing or two about buzzwords

Contents

The Buzzword Bingo Book

Buzzword Bingo:
Where did it come from?

uzzwords date back to 35000 B.C., when primitive verbal
communication limited early hunter-gatherers to simple
phrases such as "Food here" and "Food there." Even this
was an amazing achievement, since we have no reason to believe
these folks were grunting in English. Nevertheless, it was this basic
communication, plus sharp pointed sticks and large animals too
dumb to avoid the sharp pointed sticks, that allowed humans to
survive—and eventually dominate the planet.

It was a harsh, brutal time, and even with the aid of sharp
pointed sticks, the hunters occasionally failed to bring food home to
the community. In such situations, the unsuccessful hunter would
diminish in standing—perhaps even to the point of becoming the
main course of the evening meal. It was under these stressful condi-
tions that human communication took an evolutionary leap forward
with the introduction of the "buzzword." A hunter, facing the
dilemma of expressing his failure at food gathering, abandoned the

usual "Pointed stick missed" excuse and subsequent slow roasting over an open fire and instead offered, "Strategic resource management paradigm shift" with a knowing shrug of the shoulders. The community was awed by the incomprehensible string of syllables and immediately elevated the failed hunter's status to that of hero and grand poobah. And by this process of natural selection, a new class of humanity known as management was born.

From the moment of that first heady rush, management has relied on the use of clever-sounding but incomprehensible words and phrases—buzzwords—to maintain an aura of mystery and power. The more mysterious the terms, the more the manager increased his ultra-insider status in the eyes of colleagues and underlings. And the more the manager distinguished himself through the skillful use of buzzwords, the more he advanced in the organization.

Over time, though, managers and would-be managers lost touch with *why* they were using buzzwords—to advance and defend—and got hooked on the nectar of the words themselves. They got addicted to stumping colleagues with all new buzzwords or by winning the occasional buzzword "shooting match," the ultimate in verbal one-upmanship. They got dependent on the thrill of making it from one end of a sentence to another using only buzzwords—the conversational equivalent of crossing Times Square on a high wire. *Can he do it? Can he do it? YESSSSSS!* Now it's like sniffing glue— they just can't help themselves.

This addiction to buzzwords isn't pleasant to behold. In fact, the ordinary employees figured out pretty quick that they were being jerked around by the managers in love with the sound of their own buzzwords. So the rank and file decided to fight back. Their weapons were more like spitballs than Minuteman missiles. And it was more a silent underground insurrection than a violent massacre. It was a bloodless revolution that took place in the back rows of seminars and business meetings across the land. And it was called Buzzword Bingo.

The Buzzword Bingo Revolution

Knowing they were listening to drivel, lots of the regular employees just snickered to themselves as the managers and consultants spouted buzzwords for their own purposes. But Tom Davis, a Silicon Valley scientist and founder of Silicon Graphics, had a revelation. One day while staring at a blackboard covered with buzzword terms, the proverbial lightbulb flickered above his head and the game Buzzword Bingo was born. He went back to his desk and created a program that could shuffle a whole database of buzzwords and generate bingo cards filled with the terms. He handed cards out to colleagues and challenged them to play at the next meeting. Needless to say, the game was a rousing success.

Buzzword Bingo spread like a computer virus from B-school to B-school and into every nook and cranny of the corporate landscape. But it remained a somewhat anonymous, underground, interoffice survival tool until Scott Adams, of *Dilbert* fame, mentioned the game in his comic strip. Suddenly, the whispers about Buzzword Bingo became outright laughter, which on occasion broke out during a meeting. From that day on, Buzzword Bingo began to gain an avid following of rabble-rousing revolutionaries, who remained in the shadows but played the game nevertheless.

The Wall Street Journal published a front-page article on Buzzword Bingo in June 1998 and blew the lid off the thing. In an instant, everyone from the mailroom to the boardroom knew about Buzzword Bingo. And even while the people who'd long been furtively playing the game knew their cover had been blown, they laughed to know that the Emperor (management) didn't have a stitch of clothing to wear to his next "interdepartmental facilitators' meeting."

Today, Buzzword Bingo beats the pants off sleeping or multi-cocktail premeeting lunches to fend off the numbing effects of long, boring meetings. More people than ever are playing the game, making their own rules, making up their own buzzwords, and getting a darn good chuckle out of it. Which is good, because management deserves the mockery. But remember: Talking about Buzzword Bingo too much threatens to make it mainstream. So shhhhhhh. Just play.

What Is a Buzzword?

How do you know a buzzword when you hear one? There are a few characteristics found in buzzwords that are good clues you're hearing the real phony thing:

First, overuse. When you suddenly start hearing a word or phrase you've never heard before being used over and over by the boss—and then mimicked by the manager-toadies—you got yourself a buzzword. The word catches on like wildfire and is used ad nauseam in speeches, memos, official company documents, etc. Eventually, you start hearing it on the nightly news. Then, just as you begin to catch yourself using the word, it disappears from the planet due to overuse. "Information superhighway" is one of those buzzwords.

Second, misuse. Some buzzwords become buzzwords when someone starts misusing them or using them outside of their original context and they catch on like bad grammar. The word or phrase may be misused so often that no one remembers what the word meant in the first place. For example, the buzzword "algorithm." This word used to be like a pair of brown oxfords—a nice, boring, dependable mathematical term referring to any particular procedure for solving a certain type of problem, such as the rule for finding the greatest common denominator. Now MBA smarty-pants toss it around with utter disregard for its real meaning, pretty much just to imply they were once gifted students who excelled in advanced math. They use it to refer to any old process. They use it to refer to steps of any kind. Heck, they even use it as a generic placeholder in a sentence, as if it were an armrest or something. "Hey, what's the algorithm on that lunch order?"

Finally, "multi-utilizational functionality." In other words, the longer the buzzword, the more uses (and less meaning) it has. These buzzwords are used to make the speaker or writer sound intelligent and informed. And to fill the air. A great example is the buzzword "interactive feedback." The concept of feedback necessitates that there be interaction between at least two people, so isn't "interactive feedback" redundant? Of course it is. But "interactive feedback" sounds more technologically advanced than either "feedback" or "interaction" alone. Plus, it sounds more like a secret code, which is half of what makes the use of buzzwords so compelling to the goobers who use them. Here's a hint if you're thinking of using one of these yourself: The long buzzwords work better in print than in person.

Where Do the Buzzwords Come From?

Sometimes buzzwords have interesting origins, such as the word "protodigital." Jan Kellberg invented the word while studying history and security information systems in Sweden. The word was derived from the term "protoindustrial," which was used in Marxist historical materialistic theory. "Protoindustrial" refers to the workshops and manufacturers that existed between the late Renaissance and the late eighteenth century. In 1996, Jan Kellberg transformed "proto-industrial" into the new buzzword, "protodigital," which refers to the pre-stage of the digitally structured society. To slip "protodigital" into the active buzzword lexicon, Jan carefully planted the word into correspondence among those on a select mailing list, and before long, it was out there in use, as if it had been there all along.

Now, "protodigital" is the story of a deliberate buzzword plant, but more often than not, buzzwords are just more or less inadvertently borrowed terms. Buzzwords can come from just about anywhere—science and technology, business school, or sports, to name a few prime sources. You find them as headings on spreadsheets or interoffice memos. And a gold mine source of buzzwords are high-priced consultants' "leave-behinds"—those documents they hand out at the end of every meeting to prove they were there. The point is, the more creative you are in appropriating a term from somewhere else and using it like the devil until everyone's doing it, the quicker you'll become a buzzword king.

Make Your Own Buzzwords!

So how can you create your own buzzword? The easy way—the beginner's way—is to take two or three office-related terms and glue them together. Then slowly start using the phrase during key conversations or meetings and watch the word's use spread. When the word is used in a memo or E-mail that you receive (so the new word has come full circle), you're the proud parent of a brand-new buzzword. Classic buzzwords that were created in this fashion include "learning organization" and "management cost environment."

Another method of creating a buzzword is to actually fuse two terms together, such as "strategic" and "tactical." The new buzzword is "stratical," which refers to various approaches to marketing and positioning. Another example melds the words "cooperation" and "competition," forming the new buzzword "co-opetition," which refers to competitive cooperation between rivals.

Finally—and here's one of our favorites—you just brazenly pick a word, any word, and start using it in a whole new context. You must be very matter-of-fact, very nonchalant—the bolder the word choice the better. Let's make one up right now. "Fireworks." Perfect. "Fireworks" means the added attraction, the grand finale, the sparkly but not intrinsically important endnote. "You had to see it, man. When I finished the fireworks on my presentation, Stevens jumped out of his chair and shook my hand." No one will ask you what you mean by "fireworks." It will quickly become understood through its use in context, and soon someone will use it on *you*. Triumph.

Let's Play Buzzword Bingo

The simplicity of the game is in fact its genius. For starters, all you need are a few Buzzword Bingo Game Cards, which you can borrow from the back of this book or print out from the Buzzword Bingo Web site at http://www.buzzword-bingo.com. Everyone who's playing needs a game card, of course.

The Buzzword Bingo Game Card has a total of 25 squares, each containing a buzzword. The middle space, as in regular bingo, is a free square. The object of the game is to mark the buzzwords used by a meeting's talking head, aiming to mark five squares in a row—vertically, horizontally, or diagonally. First guy to get five in a row wins. How simple is that?

Once you've crossed off a row of buzzwords, you can jump up and whoop, "Bingo!" Or, if you are at all interested in keeping your job, you can adopt a more, um, discreet acknowledgment of victory. Gather the game players before a meeting and agree on a coded victory signal. For example, two loud coughs or a long arm stretch in the air would suffice to claim Buzzword Bingo dominance. The victory signal should be subtle enough to avoid detection by the meeting's speaker. To further the secret agenda, change victory signals often to keep management off your scent.

The Many Ways to Play

To keep the game fresh and exciting, there are plenty of rule variations and game options. You can add devilish restrictions or elaborate scoring systems to the game to make winning not quite as easy as just getting five in a row. First, there are variations based on the buzzwords themselves.

Certain Buzzword Phrases

Instead of using all manner of buzzwords, why not allow only a particular variety of buzzword phrases? For instance, managers love to use a strain of empty buzzword phrases, which often become signature phrases, such as "As we move forward . . ." or "At the end of the day . . ." These phrases are not business-oriented in any way or technological at heart. They're just meaningless little puffs of air that punctuate many a manager's speech. Think about the bosses in your office. They use their familiar favorites as unconsciously as blinking or swallowing.

> "The bottom line is . . ."
> "In order to grow this company . . ."
> "Our collective goal here is to . . ."
> "Let me just riff on this a minute . . ."
> "Yadda, yadda, yadda . . ."

Playing this brand of Buzzword Bingo calls for custom-made game cards, incorporating the phrases common to your company's lexicon. But that's the fun in it—cataloguing the phrases you've long known and sneered at and incorporating them into the broader Buzzword Bingo dictionary.

It's Time to Step Up to the Plate

Another buzzword-specific variation on Buzzword Bingo focuses on the use of sports terms or metaphors. Many managers use sports lingo in an embarrassing attempt to connect with the employees through a perceived common interest in sports. Additionally, managers increasingly see themselves in the role of a coach or trainer to their charges. So sports slangology pervades the workplace. Thanks to baseball, for instance, we "hit home runs" or are encouraged to "get up to bat." Sometimes things "come out of left field" and other times a much anticipated event—a new product launch, perhaps—is "rained out." We've got "holes-in-one," "hat-tricks," and "touchdowns." There are "power hitters," "utility players," and "zone defense" strategies. And thanks to sports buzzwords in the workplace, we're endlessly asked to "raise the bar" or "step up to the plate."

The mixed sports metaphor in the workplace is particularly dizzying. The following was actually heard in a weekly sales meeting: "We have so many balls in the air that if we can just get our ducks in a

row, I'm sure we can put a few points on the board . . . maybe even hit a home run or two." All this sports nonsense—it's exhausting, really.

So the sports-oriented version of Buzzword Bingo calls for special attention to be paid to the overuse of sports buzz-words. Custom-made game cards could feature just sports buzzwords. Or, even more challenging, the cards could contain buzzwords from just a single sport—all baseball buzzwords, for example. At the very least, the game cards must be sprinkled with at least five sports buzzwords each, along with the regular variety of non-sports, just-plain-dumb buzzwords. And when a player marks five in a row, he's gotta yell, "Fore!" Natch.

Unidisciplinary Buzzword Bingo

Since most office meetings revolve around a specific topic—sales projections, quarterly marketing plans, or customer support initia-tives, for example—how about tailoring the game to particular cate-gories or meetings?

The Customer Service Buzzword Bingo Game Card might over-load on terms like:

- consumercentric
- value systems
- excellence

- value constellation
- supply management

The Marketing Department Buzzword Bingo Game would stress terms such as:

- contingency planning
- co-branding
- market-based view
- infused marketing

Even more category-specific might be a game revolving around the year 2000 challenge. If you attend a meeting at which this subject is central, chances are you will hear every one of these buzzwords:

- Y2K
- year 2000 compliant
- year 2000 anxiety
- year 2000 fallout
- year 2000 implementation
- year 2000 solutions
- legacy systems
- year 2000 standards
- systems integration

Turning your Buzzword Bingo games into tighter, more subject-specific challenges can make the game more intense—and even more of an inside joke than it already is.

Using Acronyms

Acronyms are a favorite variety of buzzwords because it's even easier for managers to get away with using them and not explaining what they mean. For example, everyone is familiar with the acronyms TLC (tender loving care) and ASAP (as soon as possible), but what about BPR (business process reengineering) or ERP (enterprise resource planning)? Then there's ALARA (as low as reasonably achievable) and BATNEEC (best achievable technique not entailing excessive cost). Sick, isn't it?

Certain buzzword enthusiasts will take any three words and turn them into an acronym. For example, RIF stands for a reduction in force and SFA stands for sales force automation. It's no mystery why managers feel the need to turn all three-word phrases into acronyms—it makes conversation more of a secret code, to which only a select few are privy. As buzzwords, acronyms are essentially the next level of buzzwords—standard buzzwords made even more useless by further reduction into acronyms.

There are two ways to play Buzzword Bingo using acronyms. The first is to replace as many of the buzzwords on your game card with representative acronyms. The speaker would have to be utterly acronym-obsessed for anyone to win, but make no mistake—it's happened.

The second way to play Buzzword Bingo using acronyms is to fill in each square of a game card with individual letters. Then, as the speaker uses an acronym, cross out the individual letters of the acronym on your card. The first to cross off all of the letters on the game card wins. This Buzzword Bingo variation sounds easy, but it plays much trickier than you think, since you're quickly spelling terms out in your head, searching for the letters, and possibly missing the speaker's next acronym while hunting and pecking on your card.

Acronym game cards can be accessed at the Buzzword Bingo Web site at http://www.buzzwordbingo.com/play/acronyms.html.

Who Said What?

Finally, if you are looking to increase the challenge involved in Buzzword Bingo, randomly add a person's name to five buzzwords on each game card. Then a buzzword can only be crossed off if uttered by the proper person. This works best for collaborative meetings, where the usual management suspects are in attendance and constant discussions are the norm.

Tally the Score

Another way to up the ante on Buzzword Bingo is to bring a point
system to your game. Each buzzword is assigned a point value,
much the same way words are variously valued in Scrabble.
Determine buzzword points any number of different ways, such as
by the length of the word or the number of words in the phrase. For
example, assign 1 point per letter in each buzzword. This would
mean that "empowerment" would be worth 11 points, and "flexible
standards" would be worth 18 points.

To complicate the scoring system even further, you can issue
point values to buzzwords based on their level of incomprehensibil-
ity. In other words, the less sense the buzzword makes, the more
points that word is worth. Using a sliding scale for calculating values, devise a scoring system along these lines:

Clearly understandable	Sort of understandable	Barely understandable	What the hell does this mean?
5 points	10 points	15 points	20 points

Of course, the difficulty lies in the actual rating of each buzzword on a point scale of this nature. Who's going to be the rating-
meister? Well, there's an enterprising soul in every office—and you
know who you are—who is willing and able to create a Scrabble-
style buzzword point system to be used and enjoyed by all the
highly competitive Buzzword Bingo players. Once this scoring sys-

tem is created, it will morph and mutate and become the basis of your company's custom brand of Buzzword Bingo.

Bonus Buzzword

Another scoring variation involves the use of a Bonus Buzzword. Each player is allowed to choose one Bonus Buzzword—let's pick "leverage" for the sake of this explanation—to include at the top of his or her game card. Each time the speaker uses the word "leverage," a player makes a check mark against the word and a bonus point is earned. At the end of the boring meeting, er, game, the player adds the extra bonus points to his or her regular total score.

Buzzword Bingo Seasons

Instead of determining a winner for each game within the context of a meeting, why not play all-day Buzzword Bingo? This variation requires players to be in a heightened state of awareness so buzzwords can be picked up from meetings, telephone calls, or casual conversation.

Even more elaborate is Buzzword Bingo played over the course of a "season." Determine the length of a season—say, a week, or maybe the course of a three-day seminar. Game scores are tallied on an ongoing basis, and season standings are posted regularly. At the end of the season, the player with the most points wins.

The Play-offs

Having Buzzword Bingo play-offs can complicate a regular Buzzword Bingo Season deliciously. For example, the top four game players at the end of a season could play a semifinal set of buzzword matches, and then a final Buzzword Bingo match, to determine the season's Buzzword Bingo champion. The kind of people who play rotisserie anything will know how to blend all the variations and scoring strategies of the game to make the play-offs complicated and challenging. As good as going to the U.S. Open—and a lot cheaper.

Reverse Buzzword Bingo

Finally, let's explore an inversion of the standard Buzzword Bingo game, in which players mock the managers by playing Reverse Buzzword Bingo.

In Reverse Buzzword Bingo, the *players* attempt to use as many buzzwords from their game cards as possible while participating in a meeting. For this game to work, the meeting has to be an open discussion and not a stand-alone speech by the boss or manager. Reverse Buzzword Bingo works beautifully during a brainstorming session, for instance. The first to use and mark five buzzwords in a row on his or her card wins.

Reverse Buzzword Bingo is a particularly rewarding form of entertainment as it allows the players to bandy about buzzwords in the open while the managers are ignorant of their pawn status in the game. This game can involve extensive strategy as players work to use the buzzwords without detection, seamlessly weaving them through the course of a real meeting. Any flagrant misuse or gratuitous use (as if it weren't *all* misuse and gratuitous use!) of a term can disqualify a player. No buzzword blurting!

Someone Has to Lose

In every game there's a loser. The same goes for Buzzword Bingo, so turn up the heat. Let's make losing really hurt.

You Lose, You Use

After completing a Buzzword Bingo match, the winner of the game assigns one buzzword-laden sentence to each loser. Then at the next yawn-inspiring, management-induced meeting, the losers have to use their horrible buzzword sentence. Here follows a transcript from a meeting with the Marketing Manager (MM):

MM: Well, folks, as we approach the new millennium, we must advocate new change in our internal network of business partners. How are we going to accomplish this task?

LOSER #1: I say we implement a paradigm-shifting SFA system enabling our partners and staff to co-facilitate and co-develop new, truly stackable, and chaos-compliant products.

LOSER #2: I would have to disagree with your thoughts on this. From the market analysis I have completed with various multidisciplinary teams, I have discovered that the most coherent way toward a fast return on investment would be to implement a more diverse, forward-thinking system, allowing us to follow a user-friendly, global roll-out.

MM: Excellent points! Why don't we separate into leadership teams, follow some nonsequenced instruction, and pilot-test our new, de-conflicting developments? Waddya say?

And all the wonderful prizes!

As in life, one mustn't ignore the importance of the reward system. Free beer or late-afternoon chocolate to the winner, paid for by the losers. That's "incentivization," folks!

The Buzzword Dictionary

A Limited Selection of Some Buzzy Buzzwords, Corpo/Techno-jargon, and Workplace Slang!

1:1: Shorthand for "one-to-one marketing," as popularized by Don Peppers and Martha Rogers in their book *The One-to-One Future*. The thesis is that it's getting harder and harder to get new customers, so businesses can extract more profit by getting more money from their existing customers. "Share of wallet instead of share of market" is the mantra.

24/7: All day, every day, 24 hours a day, 7 days a week. Kinko's is a 24/7 operation. Shorthand for "I have no life."

80:20: Shorthand for the old theory that 80 percent of the work takes 20 percent of your time, and 20 percent of the work takes 80 percent of your time. It sucks, but it's true.

90% Solution: A solution that doesn't entirely resolve the problem but leaves you 90 percent sure the problem will likely come up again. *See also* "Band-Aid."

110%: What's expected, in terms of personal effort and commitment, to get the job done. Usually requires mass quantities of overtime.

404: Someone who is clueless. From the World Wide Web error message 404 Not Found, meaning that the requested document couldn't be located. "Don't bother asking him; he's 404."

Across the Organization: Companywide. Everyone in the company's employ. Usually refers to the way in which a company has to get everyone to go along with a new policy or strategy or theory. "We've got to get a commitment to this thing across the organization." Often describes the cumulative effects of a bad decision.

Action Item: The next thing on the to-do list, should you ever get out of this meeting and see the list.

Actionable: Inspiring response, retaliation, challenge, or correction. "Bonnie's behavior in that meeting was actionable; she'll get a call from HR."

Actualize: To make something come true. You actualize a plan by doing it. This would happen to you if you ever got to the action items list.

Ad-hoc: A fancy way of saying you're making things up as you go along. Use it as a verb to show off. "I ad-hoc-ed this memo."

Admin Tools: Software tools that system administrators use to tinker under the hood. Like NSLookup, which lets you look up a domain and get its IP number. Shrug.

Affiliate Program: A concept popularized by such large on-line businesses as Amazon.com, the affiliate program allows a company to expand its network of sales by getting other Web sites to send business their way. Affiliate programs pay small commissions to affiliates, though, so it's pretty much a one-way street.

Aggregate (verb): Grouping other people's resources, then leveraging them to make money. Yahoo aggregates eyeballs on-line and then directs them to places where money can be made.

ALARA: As Low as Reasonably Achievable. Cheap, cheap, cheap.

Algorithm: Originally a mathematical term for the step-by-step process for solving a problem. Now it means any tested, methodical approach to getting from A to Z. We used to call this a plan.

Alliance: After a company partners with another company, it is announced with a press release and—voilà!—an alliance. We used to call this a partnership.

Alpha Geek: The most knowledgeable, technologically proficient person in the workplace. "Ask Larry. He's the alpha geek around here." And, yes, we used to just call him a geek.

Alpha Release: First test distribution (to friends only) of near-to-final version of a new product. So if there's any broken stuff in it, there's still time to fix it before the official launch.

Ambiguous Navigation: A scenario in which there is more than one entry point and more than one exit point, so it's never entirely clear what you have to do to get from here to there. Like life.

Analysis Paralysis: The result of studying a problem in search of the perfect solution until one becomes stuck, unable to take any action until precisely the right course of action is identified. Which may be never. Can result from MBAs from different schools actually having a conversation.

Anchoring Concept: One idea that helps justify a collection of other ideas that appear to have no purpose or direction.

Annotate: To make a note in the margin, in swanky talk.

Ask the Hard Questions: To grill someone, usually about what went wrong on a project. Alternately, to ask a whole bunch of unanswerable, rhetorical questions meant to challenge and provoke. Usually the first step in identifying a scapegoat.

Asset: The "buns of steel" employee—a can-do, tireless, good-natured workhorse. "Ben's been with us for ten years; he's a real asset to this company." In other words, you can count on him to work hard until midnight without a grouse or a grumble. *See also* "enabler."

Assmosis: The process by which some people seem to succeed and advance by kissing up to the boss rather than working hard.

Asynchronous: Refers to different processes that can occur without one being completely dependent on another. A synchronous modem has to have a dialogue orchestrated between the computers on either side of the modem. This is slow and painful. On the other hand, an asynchronous modem can carry on both sides of the dialogue at once, with neither side waiting for the other, which is, of course, much faster and very similar to the sort of communication that goes on on commuter trains and at cocktail parties all across the country. Asynchronous projects "across an organization," if properly designed, would dramatically increase the speed with which stuff gets done. However, it usually leads to rapid activity, followed by even more rapid rework.

"At IBM/Microsoft/Stanford/MIT, we . . .": Pedigreed corporate veterans and alumni love to name-drop about their background. This phrase has no definition, per se, but it is a classic buzzword winner.

Attack the Problem: To attempt to solve. "Let's attack this problem from a different angle."

Available for Reassignment: How a consultant or employee who has finished a project and has to find something new to do (or end up on the street) describes himself. Lately, it's been expanded to refer to individuals who aren't necessarily finished with their project but are just plain finished. Also describes an employee not smart enough to know you should never really "finish" a project. Also known as "on the beach."

BPR: Business Process Reengineering. Turning the tables upside down and starting over.

Backload: To avoid all issues up front. Scarlett O'Hara knew how to backload.

Ball's in Your Court: A phrase used to pass the buck. The next move or decision is yours.

Band-Aid: An ineffectual, temporary solution to an ongoing problem. It may stop the bleeding, but it ain't gonna heal the wound. Something you do right before you hand off the project to the "new guy."

Bandwidth: Originally referred to the amount of data that could be squeezed through a phone line or fiber cable, but today it is a way of describing a manager's ability to deal with lots of new information, "challenges," and people. "Let's give this one to Dave. He has the bandwidth to handle it."

Barrier to Entry: An obstacle to penetrating a new market. Competitors must cook up ways to prevent their competition from horning in on the action. Effective obstacles include patents, trademarks, distribution, location, etc.

Beepilepsy: The brief seizure people sometimes have when their beeper goes off (especially in vibrator mode). Characterized by physical spasms, goofy facial expressions, and interruption of speech in midsentence. This happens to people addicted to the beep.

Benchmark (verb): In the days of craftsmen who actually had workbenches, a benchmark was a standard that would be marked on the workbench to be sure that every item made was as precisely the same length as the last one. Today, it's a way of measuring performance (of a job, a product, a service) against a known standard. One or more attempt to put a word to quantifying productivity. Simply, the person or firm doing what you do, better.

Benefit: A benefit is a clever restatement of a "feature," but from the "end user's" point of view. A manager doesn't hail the "features" of the all-nighter his group has ahead of them; he touts the benefits—the accomplishment of a job well done and the camaraderie enjoyed when a team tackles a project with a looming deadline. Plus, they get to keep their jobs!

Best in Class: A first cousin of "benchmarking," this term is a bit of braggadocio. It implies that when all features are considered, this product sets the benchmarks in its category. Of course, imaginative managers work very hard to define the class so there's essentially no competition.

Best of Breed: An employee who comes from a top Ivy League school.

Best Practices: If you can't think of a great solution, steal one! "Benchmarking" the best practices of other companies, in other industries, is a clever way to borrow the cream that's risen to someone else's surface. The big consulting firms love this one.

Best Thinking: Fresh, insightful, innovative thinking, most often the work of an employee with no power or inclination to speak up, and most often appropriated and taken credit for by the employee's most immediate manager.

Betamaxed: When a technology is overtaken in the market by inferior but better marketed competition, as in "Microsoft betamaxed Apple right out of the market."

Beta Release: Second test distribution of near-to-final version of a new product. If there are big bugs at this stage, things aren't looking good.

Big Picture: A term coined by upper management who don't like to pay attention to details, this means the larger worldview; the panorama versus just what's in front of one's face. Management looks at the big picture because it's responsible for the successful integration of the efforts of all of the elements of a company in pursuit of profit. Employees look at the big picture and see only the profits, of which they seem to get only the slightest wisp of a share.

Big Win: When the outcome is extremely positive—or at least not close to negative.

Blamestorming: Sitting around in a group discussing why a deadline was missed or a why project failed or even why a company folded—and who was responsible. Derived from "brainstorming," this is a terrific pastime in "post-entrepreneurial" environments. Coming up with a way to pin the blame on someone else is an art, not a science.

Bleeding Edge: Beyond the leading edge, the bleeding edge is so sharp that it leads to serious cuts and hemorrhaging. Usually experienced by the high-technology industry.

Block Scheduling: The act of scheduling huge chunks of time so that a day is devoid of unscheduled moments and consists of moving from one mind-numbing meeting to another. Leads to "24/7."

Boutique-style: An image of being small, highly attentive to customers, and highly creative. A boutique-style ad agency is thought to be able to create cutting-edge ads for a discerning clientele. Fancy description for a firm with a few products, fewer clients, and little revenue.

Brain Dump: A rapid debriefing of all the data on a given topic. Rarely organized; often not very useful and, unfortunately, generally occurs at 8 p.m., when your brain is full.

Brainstorm: To free-associate ideas in a group setting for the purpose of stimulating creativity. A forum for those who rarely speak and are never listened to.

Branding: Marketing efforts that are meant to leave a deliberate impression in consumers' minds. It's not just the selling of the soap—it's what the soap stands for. When done badly, resembles a hot iron being slapped on a steer.

Breakout Session: A small meeting born of a larger meeting, at which the subject of the larger meeting is to be hashed over in more detail or "brainstormed."

Break the Rules: Better to beg forgiveness than ask permission. When you "think out of the box," challenge the corporate hierarchy, and are proud to be seen as a renegade, well, you're probably breaking the rules. Opposite of "playing by the rules."

Bug: A word that's officially forbidden at some companies, a bug is an error in the design or coding of a product that causes it to fail at a promised task. The goal is to describe the bug as an undocumented feature and let it go at that.

Bullet: A very important point, usually one of many to be considered. "Let's move on to the next bullet." Initially derived from the use of bullets in written memos to define a list of points, now a bullet can come straight out of a person's mouth.

Business Casual: Dockers. Unless you wore Dockers that day, in which case it's a yellow golf sweater and lightweight wool gabardines.

Business Model: Used to be, you sold a product and you made money. "We don't need no stinkin' business models!" Today, however, with every element of a business backward—when Yahoo puts a button on Compaq's keyboard for one-touch access to its site, who pays whom?—it's vital to map out exactly how you think you're going to make a profit. That map is the business model.

Business Silo: A group within a company that believes it is able to make smarter decisions in a vacuum, rather than with input from other relevant groups. The last remaining benefactor of the org chart. The best evidence of org chart failure.

Buy In (verb): This is more than just agreement with a concept, idea, or proposal. It implies a deep moral commitment to root for the idea passionately in public—and only work to sink it in private.

Cannibalize: Launching a product that steals "market share" from one of your other products. While this sounds stupid, it's actually a clever plan. Better to put yourself out of business than to let someone else do it.

Cash Cow: A business that is a steady source of profit but isn't growing: Smirnoff vodka; Caterpillar tractors.

Cash-intensive: An initiative that's expensive right from the git-go.

Cast a Net: To make a broad, undefined, even random appeal and see what results.

Chainsaw Consultant: An outside expert brought in to reduce the employee head count, or "shake the dead leaves out of the trees," leaving top brass with clean hands. Al Dunlap, former chainsaw CEO of Sunbeam, is the poster child for this breed.

Challenges: No one has problems anymore. Problems have been replaced by "challenges," a term which is now used to keep employees relaxed and, it is hoped, to reduce stress-related breakdowns in the workplace.

Champion (verb): To gather a group of people. Or to force a group of people into a situation they would otherwise abhor or shy away from.

Change Agent: A new piece of data or external force—or even just happenstance—which means that all bets are off and your "business model" must be reevaluated. Or, "There's a new consultant in town."

Cherry Picking: Grabbing for the easy projects, which, when effortlessly completed, make the employee look like a hero.

Close the Loop: To resolve any outstanding issues or questions so that the matter can be filed away, mentally or otherwise, as finished.

Closure: Finished off. This word means exactly what you'd think, but it must be used in the right context to have any impact. "Come to closure" and "get closure" are pretty much the only ways to spin it. Unfortunately, most of us spend our days only "looking for closure."

Coaches: Offices no longer have bosses; instead, bosses are now known as coaches. This friendlier image suggests a less hierarchical, more mentorial structure, enabling employees to feel less dominated by forceful bosses. Er, coaches.

Cobweb: A Web site that never changes.

Co-create: To work in teams to invent stuff. Using this verb is a way of sharing credit—or forcing others not to hog the credit. Allows underachievers a crumb of recognition.

Cognitive Development: The prospect that the intellectually challenged can somehow catch up to the rest of us if they just work at it. The single best way to do this appears to be to hold seminars—the more expensive, the better.

Collectively as a Group: Redundant, natch, for "together."

Come on Board: To be hired.

Comfort Zone: The average level at which one can expect someone not to shriek in horror or disbelief. Sales types always try to stay within a potential client's comfort zone when floating a price.

Common Platform: The combination of an operating system, hardware, and software comprises a platform. When two or more parties engage in the use of products that are the same or compatible, they are running on a "common platform."

Connectivity: Originally a software/networking term that described how computers can work together, it's now applied to human interactions. "Martha, there's just no connectivity in your department. Maybe it's time for a retreat."

Consensus-builder: One whose gifts include the ability to convince an often disparate group of colleagues to go along with a plan. The internal politician.

Constituencies: All of the players who end up on your team. Building loyal constituencies is preferable to alienating constituencies.

Content: The information, usually represented in word form.

Content Provider: A company or individual that creates information, usually in word form.

Context: The subtle environment in which something is said. Suddenly, context is more important than content. Knowing who said something, when it was said, and who it was said to may be more important than *what* was said.

Context Switch: A context switch is required to understand how someone wearing a different pair of moccasins would experience an idea or product.

Continuous Improvement: The act of tinkering with a process endlessly. The art of mass production requires that a good process be invented and pretty much never touched again. Advocates of continuous improvement maintain that process is king and that the process must be improved at every moment.

Co-opetition: Is it possible to win by working together? Companies that form alliances for their mutual benefit can

often destroy the less reciprocal monopolists. That's
co-opetition.

Co-opt: To persuade a fellow employee, senior management, or
"end user" to choose your desired outcome by slowly
growing on and around them. Start slow, build "constituencies," offer free samples, and—finally—triumph.

Core Competency: You can't be good at everything. Companies are
blessed with some areas in which they're more compe-
tent than others, and if those areas are at the heart of
the company's business model, they must be expanded
and defended at all costs. It would enhance company
self-esteem if the phrase were "core excellences," but
that doesn't roll off the tongue as nicely.

Corporate Culture: This has nothing to do with yogurt or sourdough
bread and everything to do with the core values that
describe a company's "mission" and methods, as well
as the collective behavior that represents the values in
action. Cultures are rarely developed intentionally, but
they always take hold and can drive virtually every element of a company's future. It's the way people talk,
dress, negotiate, and interact internally and externally—

and even the way they describe themselves. The corporate culture at Microsoft is a little different than what you might find at, say, the Salvation Army.

Corporate Image: How the rest of the world perceives you. You used to be able to define a company by its products. Suddenly, the company's image is as important as the products it sells. Nike's image switched from hero and champion of the true athlete to money-grubbing dinosaur in about five minutes. It matters.

Cost-effective: Does it pay? Is it cheaper than the alternatives? Does paying the money to do it make more sense than not paying the money and not doing it? Then it's cost-effective. Much more sophisticated than "cheap."

Cost Management: Well, if you're going to go ahead and measure the cost-effectiveness of things, you need someone to manage that, don't you?

Cost-Reduction Strategies: No one is 100 percent sure what these strategies are, but constant meetings are necessary to discuss the options. By the millennium, all successful businesses will have reduced costs—or failed.

Create a New Space: To carve out a brand-new corner of a market. Products that lead their market own the space. If the space you're eyeing already has a leader, you'll have no choice but to create your own space. Nike created the new sneakers-as-athletic-fashion space, for example.

Critical Path: When the parties engaged in finishing an important project are in the home stretch, with x minutes and counting until the "drop-dead date," they are on the critical path. Everyone in the company who happens *not* to be on the critical path needs to stay the &%#$@# out of the way of those who are.

Critical Success Factor: The key element on which the success of a project or product hinges. The price point on Beanie Babies was a critical success factor.

Cross-Matrix: Like "multimedia," an onerous redundancy. A table, a graph—any such method for measuring one sort of thing against/with another.

Cross-Platform Technology: The technology required to enable disparate systems to work together. By the year 2000, everything had better be cross-platform or your systems won't properly integrate with your clients' and partners'.

Or else we could allow Microsoft to take over the world and force us to use whatever it wants. Which it's going to do anyway.

Cube Farm: An office filled with cubicles or pods. *See also* "pod palace."

Customer Retention: The keeping of a customer for the longterm. Because, as managers and marketers love to remind us, "It's a hundred times easier to sell to a current customer than to a new customer."

Customer Intimacy: More than just being on a first-name basis with the customer, this involves knowing the customer's kids' names, his favorite Chinese dish, and, more than anything, his detailed habits as a customer. Does he like to order on the 10th instead of the 15th? Does he have special delivery restrictions? Playing up one's knowledge of the customer's distinguishing characteristics (heh-heh) enhances the chumminess (and profitability) of the whole relationship.

Customizable: Having the ability to be tinkered with and adjusted in slight or significant ways, and made into a product totally honed to an individual's needs.

Dancing Baloney: Little animated GIFs and other Web F/X that are useless and serve simply to impress clients. "This Web page is kinda dull. Maybe a little dancing baloney would help."

Deck: The "hard-copy" presentation materials handed out by meeting "facilitators" as proof that a meeting took place and "issues" were discussed. McKinsey-type consultants are responsible for the panache and imagined importance of the deck. *See also* "leave-behind."

Declining Core Technology: This is similar to a "wasting asset," except that it's worse, because it's at the heart of your organization's "business model" and it's a technology, which means it's going to be "cash-intensive" to fix. In other words, you're flat out of luck by about Friday.

Decruitment: The opposite of "recruitment." Involves the systematic shedding of all the truly useful employees in a company. *See also* "uninstalled."

Deep Weeds: Serious trouble. Term derived from the fishing life, when an angler gets a lure stuck in the weeds. "If I don't get this report in by noon, I'm in deep weeds."

Deliverable: The final outcome of a manufacturing or service process. To put it simply, it's what the customer or "end user" gets. At the end of twelve hours of labor, one could describe a newborn eight-pound baby as the deliverable. Or not.

Deployment: Remember when everyone watched the space shuttle missions? They were always deploying thrusters or satellites or whatever. And don't forget the deployment of troops during the Cold War. Well, after you build a process, an initiative, or a campaign, you need to launch it. Deployments happen on "go-dates."

Desensification: What happens when you watch too many slasher movies. Or lay-offs. Or missed deadlines. You lose your ability to abhor what you see going on around you. It's what happens to management during "reorg," and it's what happens to the workforce during "downsizing." Otherwise known as "numb."

Design Considerations: Elements of a product design that are either pointless or nonfunctioning but that are preserved anyway, usually because they look cool. Nine out of ten Web sites are built around design considerations.

Design Reusability: The capacity to recycle the basic design of a product, which is disguised or slightly altered so no one knows.

Dialogue: Most businesses talk at customers and each other. Dialoguing (and this is a verb) is the approximation of actually listening and responding. To be frank, dialoguing is often a way of polling one's "constituencies" about what they want and then, finally, ignoring them.

Did You Run Purify? Have you run that critical piece of software that checks for memory leaks? "Did you run purify on that grocery list, Ma?"

Dimensionalize: As problems get more complicated, it gets ever harder to justify making quick yes or no decisions. Therefore, managers often ask to have the problem "fleshed out," and they call it "dimensionalizing the issues." Giving the dialogue some depth. This request is usually just meant to buy time.

Disconnect: One of those verbs that has become a noun, disconnect is the state of no longer actively seeking resolution or agreement. Union/management negotiations experience disconnect. Divorce court proceedings feature lots of disconnect. Any home where a teenager lives is rife with disconnect.

Discrete: The opposite of "fungible." Discrete elements of an "issue" or process are countable and separate. By breaking an issue down into its discrete components, it's easier to get a handle on the real issues.

Disincent: Jury-rigged verb form meaning "to convince someone to stop doing something." If an incentive is a compelling reason to do something, anyone can see that a disincentive is a great way to get someone to stop. "Mama grabbed away his popcorn to disincent Billy from kicking the seat in front of him."

Disintermediation: Eliminating the middlemen. Removing steps between the people who touch it first and the people who touch it last. Good luck.

Distributed System: An organization in which each component contributes to the overall efficiency of the whole. In the old days, everything was centralized. If the central mainframe got overloaded or if the VP of widgets went on vacation, everything slowed down. In a distributed system, all the other body parts are working hard and pulling their weight, so the organization hardly notices when Mr. Widgets is away at Pritikin for two weeks.

Dotted-Line Relationship: An association that is purely and highly contractual—no handshakes here.

Download: To electronically access files on another computer, usually through an on-line service or the Internet. In real life, you can also download ideas, assets, even large amounts of food from the buffet table.

Downsize: To cut financial losses by firing a bunch of people. *See also* "rightsize."

Drag and Drop: On a Mac, if you drag a file over a program icon and drop it by releasing the click button on the mouse, the file will open within the context of the program. In real life, if you drag a memo to someone else's desk, you can drop it there, but all you can do afterward is cross your fingers and hope the person will work on it.

Drill-down: To examine a concept closely, peeling back the layers to discover the ideas under the ideas. To dig deeper.

Drive: The will to overcome obstacles. Quite.

Drop-Dead Date: Deadline. The absolute last moment by which a deal must be done, a project must be completed, or a product must be shipped.

Dynamic: A force in an industry that causes a change in the business model. It sounds like dynamo and implies a lot of energy. Usually means a condition or personality whose effect was insufficiently anticipated.

Dynamic Network: A network that moves with more speed and flexibility than any regular working blockhead could possibly know what to do with.

Economies of Scale: The more you make, the cheaper your unit costs get. The first copy of a movie costs $60 million. The second print costs about $5,000. The more theaters you're in, the cheaper your average cost per theater. Pretty much means: One unit costs a lot; many units cost a lot less.

Effectual: Well, there was bound to be the opposite of "ineffectual," wasn't there? For self-esteem purposes, of course.

Ego Surfing: Scanning the Net, databases, print media, etc., looking
for references to one's own name.

Elvis Year: The peak year of popularity. For example, Barney the
purple dinosaur's Elvis year was 1993.

Embrace and Extend: Microsoft's male/benevolent philosophy
regarding outside Internet applications. Embrace them—
be their friend. Then extend them—create something
that altogether exceeds them. The kind of thing one of
Marcia Brady's snively girlfriends would have done.

Emotional Economics: The recognized (i.e., cash) value of appealing
to people's emotions in marketing.

Empowerment: To supercharge oneself or another with a false
sense of authority and intelligence. Allegedly helps to
increase self-esteem, which lasts only until the empowered person is barked at for screwing up or just plain
fired for incompetence. Truly empowered employees are
usually more effective and certainly happier.

Unfortunately, instead of actually empowering employees, managers often give them the responsibility (and the blame) but not the authority to actually do anything.

Enabler: A term used for a person who makes it easier for others to get things done. Management loves enablers. *See also* "asset."

Enabling Technology: One technology that allows another to function. You couldn't use Photoshop to edit photos until the scanner—which gets the pictures inside the computer—was invented.

Encapsulate: An old asbestos-removal term meaning to fully contain. By isolating something (or someone) in layers and layers of plastic (or people), you can limit the damage it does to everything (or everyone) around it.

End User: The consumer or client. The party who ultimately holds the product in his hands or uses the service.

Energized: Motivated by a challenge, not by money. In other words, you're not going to get a raise for that superhuman effort, but you'll sure get a wheelbarrowful of energy out of it.

Entrenched: Stagnant. Not going anywhere. "This corporate culture is entrenched; there's no room for a daring innovator like me!"

Essential: When a four-year-old begins to try to maximize her vocabulary, she starts by putting the word "very" in front of almost everything. If you're tired, after all, "very tired" must be even better. Unimaginative managers often do the same thing with the word "essential."

Essential Drivers: The critical elements that lead to success. *See also* "critical success factors."

Event Cascade: A series of incidents, one leading to the next, to some ultimate (usually negative) conclusion. All of the actions and reactions, for instance, that lead to the moment of impact in a car crash.

Event Horizon: The first incident in a series of necessarily linked incidents. The tire running over a nail in the road, which leads to the blowout, which leads to the swerving into oncoming traffic, which leads to the head-on collision with a semi. *See also* "event cascade."

Excellence: Tom Peters's "core competency." An all-purpose catch-phrase for doing things right. It's a nice word, a solid word, a word that inspires, well, excellence.

Experience Curve: How long it takes to try, try, and try again before you get it right.

Extensible: Able to be leveraged and applied to new areas. If your work is extensible, you're sitting on a gold mine.

Exit Strategy: Usually reserved for high-level management, this refers to the employee's escape plan, allowing for maximum severance and benefits, as well as a pretty sure thing of a subsequent high-paying job. Also refers to a start-up's worst-case scenario, where the investor money dries up, hopes for an IPO disappear, and the "start-up artist" needs to figure out how to get out of Dodge before the waiter brings the check.

Extract: A fancy word for "suck." You extract profits when you see them (if you're smart) and you extract value from existing assets. Same difference.

Extranet: A fancy name for a Web site with which salespeople and customers can interact.

Eye Candy: Stuff that's snazzy and visually appealing but not terribly nutritious intellectually. High-priced Web site designs have plenty of eye candy.

F2F: Face-to-face. In person. *See also* "facetime," "real time," and "RL."

Facetime: Actual time spent in the physical presence of another, as opposed to interaction conducted electronically, by telephone, or on paper. *See also* "F2F," "real time," and "RL."

Facilitate: One would imagine that it means to help organize or to create an environment in which others can make something happen, but in the end—and in real life—it usually means doing something yourself. Not to be confused with "facilitator," whose job it is to make it possible for people to do what they have to do. Or they're fired.

Facilitator: A less managerial and more supervisorial word for "coaches," "mentors," or "bosses." A facilitator handholds employees through their tasks, acting almost like a baby-sitter. "Can I get you some milk with those cookies?"

Fault Tolerance: No, this term does not refer to a soft boss who doesn't mind mistakes. Instead, it's the characteristic of a system that won't fail regardless of what happens to the machinery that's running it.

FC Release: Next-to-final (or if it all goes well, truly final) version of new product. If there are bugs in this one, the last guy to touch it is fired.

Feature: Any component of a "process" or product that is there for a purpose. And when a feature works, a "benefit" results.

Feedback: "So tell me, um, what do you think?" Heartily solicited, freely given comment on one's work or progress. Feedback is absolutely critical when dealing with customers, clients, bosses, or partners.

Fixed in the Next Release: If a new product is released and a flaw managed to make it through to the initial launch of the product, the company explains that the flaw will be removed in the next version of the product, or it will be fixed in the next release.

Flatten: To smooth the bumpy or irregular layers of an organization or a problem to a regular, manageable level.

Flesh Out: Fully develop. Usually refers to ideas, concepts, or proposals. "Let me flesh this thing out a bit, then get you a memo on it."

Flexible: When faced with a difficult problem with no obvious solution, or with a rapidly changing environment, managers can always choose a multiple-choice—or flexible—solution, which allows them to make it up as they go along.

Flexible Technology: Technology that will bend to the physical force or mental will of a superior being. An example is the 5 ¼" floppy disk.

Flight Risk: An employee who is suspected of planning to leave the company. Signs include uncharacteristically snappy dressing (for interviews), uncharacteristically long hours at the office (working up a résumé, E-mailing, and using

the telephone to get a new job), and unusually frequent
"doctor's appointments" (off-site interviews).

Footprint: An impression or contribution. The "high-priced consultant's footprint on the project was negligible."

Force Management: Like it sounds. Painful, square-peg-in-a-round-
hole management approach that refuses to take into
account changing circumstances, and instead bends circumstances to suit the management itself. Ouch.

Forecast: To make a measured bet on what's going to happen.
Good luck.

Franking Privileges: The free use of the company's postage and
delivery services for personal purposes.

From the Ground Up: The opposite of a "top-down" solution to a
problem. Usually means taking something (or a group of
someones) apart and putting it back together again.
Because it just plain wasn't working before.

FTP (verb): Originally short for "File Transfer Protocol," which defines the method you use to download a file over the Internet. Now it's an action verb. "FTP that file to me, will ya?"

Functionality: The features that work.

Functionality Freeze: The moment when it becomes clear you've added too many features to whatever you're building and now you have to get busy fixing what's broken.

Fungible: The opposite of "discrete." Water is fungible—you deal with it by the quart, not by the molecule. It's the view of all things as mass-type quantities rather than as individuals. Some managers regard employees as fungible.

Funnel It Down: Distill it, baby.

Future Gazing: Analyzing future trends. Trend analysts and experts on the future are just one step short of being fortune-tellers. They analyze events that occur more slowly than we can see them—things that will be "impacting" an industry or business ten years down the line. By this point, of course, your check is cashed and they're long out of town.

Gatekeeper: The organization or individual that controls a precious resource or a portal. This can be the receptionist with the washroom key or the supervisor with approval over ordering floppies or the division head who decides year-end bonuses.

Gating Factor: The possible delays that might keep you from finishing your project on time which you need to take into account. Think of a boat working its way through the Panama Canal: It can only go as fast as the gates in front of it open.

Generica: Features of the American landscape that are exactly the same no matter where one is: malls, airports, fast food joints, subdivisions. "We were so lost in Generica, I actually forgot what city we were in."

Geographically Dispersed: Spread out over hither and yon—as Grandma used to say.

Get a Handle On: To figure out how to think about. Commonly used expression when buying time to collect one's thoughts. "Let me get back to you after I get a handle on these sales figs."

Get Off the Dime: To quit procrastinating or avoiding address. Usually used as a firmly worded missive: "If we don't get off the dime on this, our quarterlies are going to look like crap."

Get One's Ducks in a Row: To line each problem (or "action item") up, one by one, so you can shoot 'em down one at a time. Don't tell PETA.

Get Points: To receive credit. "Smith, your report sucked, but it was on time; you get points for that."

Get Your Input: Ascertain your response. And then pretend I'm going to factor it into my own thinking and plans.

Global Fix: A correction that cures a recurring error across the board.

Globalization: If it won't sell over here, maybe we can sell it to the Chinese! Or take it to Europe and charge more for it! To do business around the globe. Requires describing your business as a "transcontinental enterprise." Personal globalization involves dating people from other lands.

Global Strategy: A plan to take over the world. Usually initiated by a megalomaniac—the one who got pummeled on the playground every day in elementary school.

Go-date: The start or launch date of a project or product. You miss your go-date, you're fried.

Go Forward: Start. Because three syllables are better than one.

Go Live: To officially launch a service or site. "I need that copy proofed and ready because we're going live on Friday."

Go-to-Market Strategy: After a product has been "ideated" and "incubated," it has to be sold. The carefully chosen pathway from the factory to the customer.

Goal Congruence: When all the individuals working on a project "buy in" to clearly stated goals and "deliverables," you've got goal congruence.

Goal-oriented: Hard-driving organizations often define themselves as goal-oriented to distinguish themselves from hierarchy-oriented, old-style companies. In other words, it's not about the structure—it's about the measurable success.

Going Forward: Also known as "moving ahead." Pretty much just means that no matter what's happened before a given moment, anything that happens next is a whole new ball game. Usually used as a term to suggest that the slate is clean, the air is clear, and everyone's ready for the next step.

Going Postal: Flat-out losing it in front of everyone. Unfortunate reference to history of postal employees who have snapped and gone on workplace shooting rampages.

Gold-star (verb): 1. To overachieve. 2. To lavish praise upon someone who overachieves.

GOOD Job: A get-out-of-debt job. A well-paying job someone takes in order to pay off debts, one that she will quit as soon as she is solvent again.

Ground-Level Action: A bottom-up or mid-level attempt to change an organization without direct intervention from above. The opposite of "top-down."

Groupware: Software is usually designed to be worked on by one person at a time. Groupware (which still doesn't actually work) is supposed to enable teams to simultaneously work together, each member on his own computer.

Guesstimate: A not necessarily educated approximation.

GUI: Short for "Graphical User Interface." A computer format that uses windows and menus and icons on a screen to enable a user to point and click on a word or image instead of using keyboard commands. Also known as a Gooey.

Hard Copy: A document that exists in paper form, as opposed to electronic or virtual forms.

Have a Lot on One's Plate: To be overwhelmed with too much (and too-varied) work. A good excuse for turning down an additional assignment. "I'd love to help, but I've got a lot on my plate right now."

Heritage: Baggage. A company's "corporate culture," combined with its "core competencies," its "corporate image," and its real history, combine to create a heritage.

Heterogeneous System: A system comprised of a bunch of different and diverse components. Picture Macs, PCs, Wintel—all living together under one roof. And working.

High Dome: An egghead, scientist, Ph.D., or otherwise rarefied expert.

Hollywired: The impending mega-marriage of interactive technology and the entertainment industry. *See also* "Siliwood."

Homogeneous System: A system comprised of similar components. An all-Mac shop.

Hot Button: An issue that is more sensitive than others.

Hyperarchy: Excessive office hierarchy. Hyperarchy exists when there are at least twenty levels from receptionist to CEO.

Idea Hamsters: People who always have their idea generators on hyper-drive. Good for "brainstorming" meetings.

Ideate: To brainstorm, but in a more thoughtful and high-powered way. Picture a brainstorming session that features a swanky catered lunch.

Illuminate: To make clear enough for everyone to see and understand.

IMHO: Short for "in my humble opinion." Precedes a claim that suggests you know exactly what you're talking about, that what you're about to say is certainly true, and above all, that you're not responsible for it under any circumstances.

Impactful: Influential to the market or the company in a measurable way. A good presentation can be impactful, and so can a new government regulation. "The tobacco company settlements were highly impactful on the industry." The swine.

Implement: It's more than just doing something. In any case, it sounds harder, so you get more points when you pull it off.

In the Know: Also referred to as "in the loop." Access to information of the most privileged sort.

In the Loop: Included in the distribution of the most sensitive, classified, or just plain newsy information. Opposite of "out of the loop."

Incent: To elicit a desired behavior by offering a reward.

Increased Communication: More meetings. More memos. More
E-mail. More office gossip. More water cooler
discussions. More communication.

Incubate: To set aside (usually an idea or project) and allow to lie
dormant until such time as a sufficient number of management types get behind it. If an idea has incubated
long enough and enough people have forgotten its ori-
gin and then it is raised again at a much later date to
great acclaim, one can take credit for the idea as new.

Ineffectual: This strategy just ain't workin', son. Next!

Information Deficit: More data required.

Infrastructure: The technical and organizational capacity to do business. Sprint has the infrastructure to handle 1 million
simultaneous calls.

Infuse: To inject, to fill to the gills. Ads can be infused with emo-
tion. Presentations can be infused with enthusiasm.
Down-for-the-count "start-ups" can be infused with cash

by investors, which may only prolong the agony. And increase the debt.

Initiative: The gutsiness to advance a new idea or have an original thought and say it. The idea itself is also an initiative.

Institutional Rigidity: Inflexibility. And pretty much redundant, in that once you've got an institution, with a hierarchy and entrenched culture, calcification sets in as the organization exercises its natural instinct to preserve itself.

Integration: No schoolbuses are involved, but it does require mixing multiple groups or processes that aren't necessarily eager to work togther. The most difficult part of most corporate initiatives is the integration of the various people and technologies involved.

Intellectual Property: If you can't touch it but it's worth something, it's intellectual property. This includes things that are trademarked, copyrighted, and patented.

Interactive: Requiring one to actually do something in response to something else. Contrary to popular belief, being interactive does not require that you touch anything.

Interactive Feedback: Can there be any other kind? The redundancy of this term makes it especially useful for unknowing, unmotivated, nonproductive managers, who love to sound knowing, motivated, and productive.

Interface (verb): Communicate. "Why don't we interface about this at an all-expenses-paid lunch tomorrow?" Current culture people prefer E-mail and avoid one-on-one contact. This is an attempt to get people to start talking to each other again.

Internet: If you want your stock to go up or wish to explain why a project is not making money, invoke the Internet.

Interoperable: The condition in which two or more diverse systems are able to get along.

Intranet: Just like the Internet, but more expensive to install and maintain, and only available internally to employees, who will probably never use it the way it was intended.

Intrapreneur: Someone too aggressive to be a team player yet not gutsy enough to actually go out and start a business of his own. So he acts like a cowboy entrepreneur within the confines of a traditional corporate environment and pretty much just pisses people off.

Issues: Unresolved matters. Unfinished business. Problems. *See also* "challenges."

Just in Time: An inventory system that provides the right part at just the moment it is needed in the assembly process, so there's no stockpiling or warehousing. If the part isn't perfect, the entire assembly line stops. A just-in-time inventory system is meant to force quality back through the system to its start. *Kanban* in Japanese. The art of lowering the water in a stream until you can see where the rocks are.

Keyboard Plaque: The disgusting buildup of dirt and crud and soda spillage found on computer keyboards.

Killer Apps: In the history of the personal computer, those programs that come around once in a while and totally redefine the way people use a computer—a word processor, a database, or E-mail, for example. Now, of course, the term refers to just about anything with superior, awe-inspiring uses.

Knowledge Management: The manager's challenge of actually knowing what her charges are up to and whether they're doing their jobs properly.

Lay-down: The initial stock offering to the inner circle of investors when a company goes public.

Lean and Mean: Stay healthy; stay edgy. Most people who are trying to get thin by dieting are in a permanently lousy mood. This mentality seems to be desirable in the cutthroat world of business.

Learning Curve: The more you do something, the better you get at it. The amount of time between when you first began gathering information or skills and when you've mastered something. Commonly used as follows: "Driving down the learning curve," or, "working our way down the learning curve." In other words, if you are described as still working up the learning curve, you're in bad shape.

Leave-behind: A piece of paper or document left behind at an off-site meeting, which is meant to remind the party both that you were there and of the subject of your discussion. *See also* "deck."

Legacy: The super-great ideas of yesterday are today's legacies. Well, even the dud ideas of yesterday are today's legacies. The trick is to make sure you're working with the right kind of legacy before you start stripping it for parts.

Level Playing Field: An alleged and elusive scenario whereby one party has equal footing with another, with neither having an edge over his competitor.

Leverage: Once you've got an asset, the challenge is to apply resources to make it even more valuable. You can leverage your education, your relationships, even a trip to California—just by figuring out some way to get more out of it.

Lightweight: Not to be taken seriously. "I don't care how much venture capital she's raised, she's a lightweight."

Litmus Test: A quick test to discover the truth. Projects have to pass the litmus test, the "smell test," and the mandatory eye exam before being implemented.

Locked and Loaded: Too late in the process to change. After a project is set or a product is ready to go to market, it's a guided missile, in full countdown mode, standing by for launch.

Low-Hanging Fruit: The easy tasks that employees get done quickly in an effort to impress the boss. *See also* "cherry picking."

Major Players: Every industry has companies that are the equivalent of the cool kids' group in high school. You know you've made it when individuals at other companies refer to you as a major player in the industry. Your company can be worth no more than the paper your stock options are written on, but if you work hard enough on presence and style, you can still be a major player.

Make It Happen: Do it. "Okay, I've signed off on your proposal. Now make it happen."

Make It Live to the World: To formally launch. *See also* "go live."

Management Style: A manager's trademarked approach to moving the pieces around on the board. Tough but fair. "Consensus-builder." Slash and burn. These are management styles.

Map (verb): To target. When Sally maps the market, she targets potential customers.

Market-driven: Determined by what the consumer really wants as opposed to what the manufacturer or service provider thinks he needs.

Marketplace Scenarios: To look into the near future and claim to know what will happen. It's more like a great big If.

Massively Parallel: If a road with two lanes moves more traffic and moves it faster than a road with one lane, think how much traffic could be moved, and how quickly, on a road with, say, a hundred lanes. If the traffic on the one-hundred-lane road represents a company's productivity, then the company could be described, admiringly, as massively parallel.

Media-rich: Loaded with sound or images or other doodads besides the written word.

Mentor: Friendly, alternative moniker for boss. Your boss is your mentor if he's showing you more attention than anybody else—for whatever reason. *See also* "coach."

Metrics: Tom Peters says that if you measure something, it will get done. Metrics are the measurement tools. You can't have a metric, of course, unless you define it. Hence the idea of clearly defined metrics, far more powerful than just a metric. Huh?

Micromanage: To single out an employee or a task or project and become overly involved in its progress, almost always with negative results. If you micromanage and succeed, you're seen as a hands-on manager. If it turns out otherwise, well, you're a micromanager.

Microplug-in: Anything you plug in to an application to extend its features and functions. Enhancements.

Middleware: Software that lets software talk to software. No human contact necessary.

Milestone: A moment or event that marks progress. A fiftieth birthday is an important milestone. So is a first million-dollar sale.

Mind Share: The workplace version of the telekinetic Vulcan Mind Meld, whereby two or more employees are electronically rigged up to transfer knowledge and information. Managers are hyped on mind share, which is critical to their "paperless office" campaigns.

Mission: The goals and objectives a company pursues with religious ferocity and devotion. *See also* "mission from God."

Mission-critical: 1. Vitally important to the accomplishment of one's mission. "I need the color printer for the rest of the afternoon—it's mission-critical." 2. When you ship a product with a component that can make or break the way that product functions, that component is mission-critical. The on/off switch on a vacuum cleaner, for example, is far more mission-critical than that little hook that holds the cord in place.

Mission from God: A maniacal pursuit of an end. Think Blues Brothers. Or the entire cast of *It's a Mad, Mad, Mad, Mad World,* especially Ethel Merman.

Mission Statement: A company's Lord's Prayer. Not even slightly related to its mission, if it has one.

More Bang for the Buck: The wringing of more value or profit or exposure from an effort. "If we run an ad in the *Post* during the Monicagate scandal, we'll get more bang for the buck."

Motivation: Pure gluttony of the soul, whereby a manager or boss fills an employee with a false sense of hope and accomplishment. *See also* "empowerment."

Mouse Milking: Going through tremendous effort for a minute amount of benefit. The point being, you can milk a mouse, but is it really worth it?

Multitasker: Someone with the ability to divide his brain to give attention to more than one task at a time.

Mutually Beneficial: Both parties win; no one gets screwed. Or everybody gets screwed but a great spin doctor makes both parties feel as if they won.

Neophyte: Someone who is new to the scene. *See also* "newbie."

Net-Net: The "bottom line"; what really matters. After deducting all the extraneous issues, what's the real issue?

Net Out: How things turn out in the end. "I'm not sure how this job's going to net out, so I'm working up my exit strategy right now."

Network: To make a strong effort to meet people and then use those acquaintances to advance one's own agenda or to get a new job.

Newbie: Green and clueless. Someone with not a whit of experience.

No-brainer: A seemingly obvious choice or course of action.

Non-sequenced Instructions: Instructions given in a backward or mixed-up order, the result being that the employee has no clue how to properly complete a task.

Objective: One's most immediate target. Can't be mission-oriented without goals; can't be goal-oriented without objectives.

Obligating Question: When a salesperson removes all possible objections to buying, the prospect is finally pressed with the obligating question: If I've satisfied all your needs, requests, and reservations, will you buy? The obligating question is a useful persuasive form for other pursuits, such as talking a romantic prospect out of his or her knickers.

Off-line: Not a part of group discussion. In private; off the record. "Could you excuse us? I'd like to take this off-line for a moment."

Off-load: To divest oneself of information; to debrief.

Off-site: A meeting so impossibly boring it has to be held outside of the office so no one can leave and go back to his desk.

On Board: Signed up, hand raised, bought in. A real team member. Or brainwashed into being a believer.

On the Beach: When a consultant is between projects and no longer earning income for the firm, she's on the beach. Her immediate goal is to get off it, fast.

On the Cutting Edge: To be out front in terms of style, technique, technological advancement, popularity, and the like. Chris Rock is on the cutting edge; Milton Berle is not.

Open System: A totally transparent, nonproprietary system that's there for the world to use, examine, and copy. Microsoft owns Windows. Apple owns the Macintosh. But no one owns UNIX. With an open system, a programmer can see how it works and, more important, can count on multiple providers to always be there.

Open-Door Policy: The suggestion that employees are heartily encouraged to drop in at any time to discuss a problem with management—except when the manager is on the phone, pretending to be busy making "mission-critical" decisions. A worker who takes this offer to heart and drops in to chat with the boss is usually treated with great suspicion by co-workers.

Operational Excellence: A special kind of excellence in which the processes used are exceeding all available "benchmarks." "Hey, this is working better than we thought!"

Operationalize: To make a new idea or process a part of a company's mainstream operation.

Opportunity: The company's chance to score a big hit—or not. In the old business days, every day was a chance to score, in a one-brick-at-a-time sort of way. Now companies strategize to be ready for their big Netscape-type opportunity. *See also* "window."

Opt In: A process in which consumers or employees raise their hands and volunteer to participate. You can opt in to voluntary sexual harassment training or to the American Airlines Frequent Flier program. Will they one day be known as "Multiple Opt In Tests"?

Organic Growth: Growth not by acquisition. While drinking carrot juice can lead to organic growth, this phrase usually refers to growth that is self-funded (with no banks or venture capitalists) and that usually relies on current (not additional) employees.

Organizational Information Base: Every piece of paper in the whole bloody office.

Org Chart: Short for "organizational chart," or a company's hierarchical, dysfunctional family tree.

Out of Pocket: Not in the office, or generally unavailable to help because of a competing "mission-critical" assignment.

"I'll be out of pocket till tomorrow morning; just leave a message on my voice mail."

Out of the Loop: Not even slightly privy to inside information.

Outperform: Exceed expectations. Way, way better than *underperform.*

Outsource: If someone else can do it faster and cheaper and better, hire her to do it. Outsource it.

Paperless Office: A hypothetical vision of an office with no paper. The idea is that everything that exists on paper can just as easily (and more neatly) exist in an invisible electronic form. Lovely idea but for the part where real life (crashes, lost files, fried hard drives, etc.) intervenes.

Paradigm: Perhaps the king of all buzzwords, but important nonetheless. When the rules of a business model change, the way to succeed changes. New rules; new results.

Partner (noun): 1. A business or associate with whom you have formed a working relationship. 2. An employee. The term "employee" is no longer effective in defining the relationships between "coaches" and their underlings. Therefore, employees are now called partners.

Partner (verb): To hook up with another company, usually on a project-by-project or product-by-product basis, the result of which is a strategic alliance. To partner is not to merge.

Pass the Baton: To hand the reins of responsibility off to another person. Sounds more elegant than it is. Usually means shoving a stack of files off your desk and on to the next sucker's.

Passion: What the managers want from the managed; what the managed usually don't get paid enough to have.

PEBCAK: Tech-support shorthand for "Problem Exists Between Chair and Keyboard," poking fun at the clueless users who call with frighteningly stupid questions.

Percussive Maintenance: The fine art of whacking the crap out of an electronic device in an attempt to get it to work again.

Permission: A simple yet sophisticated marketing concept which allows that consumers will agree—give permission—to receive and pay attention to marketing information in exchange for selfish benefits they are happy to receive. Frequent fliers are happy to pore through the voluminous marketing materials sent by the airlines in exchange for the obvious benefit of free flier miles.

Perot (verb): To quit unexpectedly, as in: "My cellular phone just peroted."

Pilot Error: Sometimes the plane crashes because the wing falls off. More often, it's because the pilot screws up. That's pilot error.

Ping: To contact someone to remind him you want an answer or a deliverable. It's nagging, really, and usually done by voice mail or E-mail.

Platform Agnostic: A person who does not believe in either UNIX or NT as being the gods of the digified earth.

Play by the Rules: To follow corporate protocol in all things. To avoid end-running or making waves or "reinventing the wheel." To play by the rules is to be a nearly transparent employee.

Portal: The supremely advantageous opening. The goal is to be the only "gatekeeper" in front of a much desired portal (like Saint Peter and heaven) and then using corporate power to leverage that position to near monopoly profits. One word: Microsoft.

Postentrepreneurial: An enterprise ceases to be entrepreneurial (hence, it is postentrepreneurial) when it (1) has more employees than customers and (2) has more meetings than new ideas. Employees who were "there in the beginning" are made sick to their stomachs as the company moves to postentrepreneurial status. Then they quit.

Postmortem: After a project fails, the postmortem presents the answer to the question Why? Usually takes the form of a formal meeting or memorandum, and is certainly preceded by one or more "blamestorming" sessions. Plus lots of bitter back-stabbing by E-mail.

Prairie Dogging: A sudden or startling disturbance, such as an argument or a dropped piece of equipment, causing heads to pop up over the "cube farm" dividers to see what's going on. Also the sudden disappearance of visible heads when trouble is brewing, such as when management arrives to deliver bad news or to dress someone down.

Price Point: Those little numbers on the price tag. What's it cost?

Proactive: The type of behavior that doesn't wait for or need a response. Instead, it pushes the issue and leads the discussion in the desired direction.

Processes: There are no more events, just processes, which are strings of related events. Marketing is a process. So is management. And your product development. And your career.

Productize: Everything that used to be a product is now a service. Television, for example, is not a box—it's a monthly cable bill. If you can figure out a way to turn a unique service into a product that can be sold multiple times to multiple customers, profits go through the roof. And once you've turned something into a service, the challenge is to leverage that effort by turning it back into a product!

Proof-of-Concept: A prototype. Even if everyone agrees an idea is a good one, it's often necessary to actually build it—just once—to see how it works.

Proposition: An expensive "action item" that management must approve before allocating resources.

Proprietary: It's mine—so don't even think about stealing it. Ideas can be proprietary; so can proposals or product proto-types. "Proprietary" is a word used to suggest lawsuits in the future of anyone who might purloin even a comma.

Protocol: A fancy process; a proven, inviolable set of steps to get something done right. A lot more precise than an "algo-rithm," but also less flexible.

Push Authority Down the Pyramid: Empowering managers often try to share authority with the grunts down in the trenches. But they often find that folks down there don't want the authority. Thanks anyway.

Put the Genie Back in the Bottle: Reverse the effects of. For instance, after some troublemaker in an industry wrecks a business model by handing stuff out free, the challenge is to somehow persuade consumers, who've gotten used to getting stuff free, that they should pay money for it again. E-commerce has let loose a buncha genies.

Quality Gaps: Minor problems that cause a product to break down, explode, or just plain disintegrate. The term is synonymous with "complete screw-up," and is used to soften the reality of another disastrous product launch.

Quantify: Measure. Some people believe that if you can't quantify it, it isn't there.

Quarterlies: The reports generated at the end of every quarter to measure all kinds of stuff, from sales to productivity to costs. Quarterlies exist as an endless reminder that you're accountable, at the very least four times a year, for what you sell and do and spend. *See also* "year-ends."

Query: A fancy way to say "question." Computers query each other all the time, and this word is usually used when one or more of the parties is inanimate.

Raise the Bar: Raise the standards and expectations to make the challenge more difficult. An excuse to get people to do more. Derived from the term for the incremental increase in the height of the high-jump bar in track and field.

Ramp Up: A very aggressive approach to accomplishing a group task. Reminiscent of the rallying of troops before battle, and therefore related to the motivation and empowerment of a workforce.

Rapid Deployment: Fast mobilization of resources.

Rathole: A small, dirty, dark place where problems go to live. And the longer they live there, the worse they get.

Reengineer: To redesign organizations and processes from beginning to end to dramatically decrease inefficiencies. In theory.

Real Estate: In the old days, it referred to land. Today, it refers to your mental "footprint" (how much attention you have from prospects) or the amount of screen space you have on Yahoo—or just about anywhere else. It's the space, real or virtual, that you occupy.

Real Time: Something that is happening right now, in person, is happening in real time. "Let's get together at ten o'clock, real time." *See also* "facetime," "F2F," and "RL."

Reality Check: A literal or figurative smack on the head. Meant to rattle someone just enough to cause a brief spurt of heightened brain activity.

Reciprocity: Sometimes known as "fairness." What's in it for the other guy?

Red Flag: Evidence that disaster or danger is on the horizon. "The dismal P&L was a red flag for the struggling sales team."

Reference (verb): To turn one's attention to. "Please reference Dave's memo on not using company E-mail for personal reasons." Dave, the bootlicker.

Regression Test: To work backward in an analysis of what leads to the outcome you seek. If you look at enough data, you can discover a road map leading to the behaviors you want.

Release (verb): Products used to be launched; now they're released.

Reorg: Short for "reorganization." No one comes out the other end of reorg happy. The state most new media and technology companies are in "24/7."

Resource-constrained: Out of time, out of money.

Revector: To change directions, in fancy *Lost in Space* talk.

Revenue-generating: The most beloved adjectival phrase in business. Means moneymaking, either by sales or cost-cutting.

Revolutionary: Adjective describing something that used to be cutting-edge or "state-of-the-art." If someone describes something as revolutionary, you can be pretty sure the revolution is old news.

Rich: Enhanced.

Rightsize: A happier word choice than "downsize." but it also means to lay off workers as a cost-cutting measure.

Risk Management: Otherwise known as damage control. Someone has to cover the boss's butt.

RL: Short for "real life." Actual, nonvirtual, non-time-zone-distorted experience. *See also* "facetime," "F2F," and "real time."

Robust: A classic buzzword that describes a product, process, event, or proposition that is well thought out and complete.

Roll Out a Server: To add computer muscle when the demand for a Web site increases. To bring in the computer server equivalent of the National Guard.

Roll-up: The entrepreneurial strategy of buying up a bunch of small companies within an industry and then going public.

Scalable Technologies: Systems that can deal with an increase in demand without a hiccup.

Scope: Depth, width, and reach. "What's the scope of commitment you're looking for?"

Scope Creep: When a project gets bigger and more sprawling, imperceptibly at first.

Script (verb): To write out all the steps. Computers will run themselves if properly scripted.

Seamless: The way all managers fantasize life could be: smooth and complication-free.

Segment (verb): To break into pieces. "Let's segment the 'challenges' here and break up into groups to 'brainstorm' them."

Self-Fulfilling Prophecy: When things come true just because everyone expects them to. Usually in the bad way.

Self-Manage: What happens when you act like you're the CEO of your own desk. Born of total disregard for the rest of the organization and how it is managed.

Self-paced: Do it at your own speed, but get it done tomorrow.

Senior Management: No matter where you are in the organization, senior management is the people above you.

Shake the Dead Leaves Out of the Trees: To identify the personnel who are underperforming and fire them.

Share of Market: Market share is the percentage of available dollars in your field that goes to your company. Intel has an 80 percent share of market in the chip biz. Or some ungodly figure like that.

Share of Wallet: The percentage of money you get from each of your hard-earned customers. When Kinko's sells you copies, office supplies, computer workstation time, and greeting cards, it is working hard to increase its share of your wallet.

Shared Space: Competitors' peaceful cohabitation within a market.

Signage: Informational indicators directing users or consumers to do, try, or buy. "Can't they do something about that Web site's signage? It's butt-ugly."

Siliwood: The coming convergence of movies, interactive TV, and computers. Also known as "Hollywired."

Site-based: This is the opposite of a "virtual organization." No wires, no shuttles, no long distance—it's right there. With actual people and meetings and memos.

Skill Set: The stuff you are good at. Or the stuff your company's good at. "Charlie's assistant has a great skill set."

Skinny on the Digit: Not pulling one's financial weight. "Fenstruck in sales has been skinny on the digit for months."

Smartsize: A euphemism for the euphemisms "downsize" and "rightsize." The subtle distinction being that if you fire a bunch of people, but hire one effective new one, you've smartsized.

Smell Test: Not a test, really, but a good, hard, close, squinty-eyed look at a situation (or a deal or a spreadsheet) to see if everything's on the up and up. You're sniffing it to see if it stinks.

Smoke Test: The early-stages test of a product or idea that determines its chances of ever seeing the light of day. If no smoke's coming from under the hood after this test drive, things are looking up.

Socialize the Idea: To try out a new idea on a handful of people in order to get people thinking friendly thoughts about it.

Softball: To make projections easier on the budget or schedule. "Oh, please. I softballed that 'drop-dead date' in case those boobs in the contract department screwed it up."

Soup to Nuts: The whole menu. A company likes to be able to offer a full-service, one-stop-shopping experience to its customers, where they can get everything from soup to nuts.

Source Control: The careful attention paid to who has the last, fully revised, fully approved, and final version of a document (or any other thing that may have many contributors' fingerprints on it). If there's no source control, then an early, unexpurgated version of the item may end up in general circulation. Which is bad.

Span of Control: The number of people reporting to a manager. Some companies want tall and thin pyramids, with every manager managing just a few people—a narrow span of control. Other—flatter—organizations prefer a wide span.

Speak to an Issue: Also known as "talking to an issue." It's really not speaking *to* anything; it's talking *about* a matter at hand. Kind of an in-line vs. on-line thing.

Spin-off: When the "intrapreneurs" in an existing company finally annoy-lienate senior management, an obvious solution is to split off the offenders into some kind of misbehaving sibling company and profit at the same time. This new company is the spin-off.

Spin: Prechewed analysis of past events that is designed to make it more likely for the recipient to draw the conclusions that the spinner desires.

Squirt the Bird: To transmit a signal to a satellite. Eew.

Start-up: A new company, started from scratch.

Start-up Artist: The new-style entrepreneur with the attention span of a gnat. He's hardly finished launching one hot-doggy new venture when he loses interest and moves on to the next.

State of the Art: The current cutting edge—which lasts about a minute.

Step Up to It: To be prepared to meet the challenge.

Strategic Planning: As opposed to nonstrategic planning? This redundancy is meant to suggest planning done with the future in mind. Now, *that's* snappy thinking.

Stratical: Describing something that's both strategic and tactical. The geographic placement of every new Wal-Mart or Home Depot is stratical.

Streamline: To eliminate the fins, obstructions, extra steps, and rough edges so as to make something go faster.

Stress Puppy: A person—staff or management—who seems to thrive on being stressed-out and whiny.

Stretch Goal: People (and companies) don't like to miss their publicly stated goals, so they have a tendency to "softball" their announced commitment even while they secretly create stretch goals, which are unrealistic, go-for-it marks. Managers then work as hard as they can to make these stretch goals the real goals. And of course Who's on first.

Structural Constraints: Stuff you can't do because senior management, physics, the government, or past mistakes won't allow you to. It's just the way it is.

Suite of Tools: The range of methods one can adopt to solve a problem or complete a task.

Sweat Your Assets: To work everything you've got—personnel, computers, the cleaning crew—really hard.

Sweet Spot: The portion of a market or a business in which profits are maximized.

Synergy: Until "paradigm" came along and kicked its butt, this one was the king of the buzzwords. It means "good overlap."

Synthesis: Combining two or more urgently contemporary ideas and creating something brand-new. MTV plus cops brought us *Miami Vice*. Such as it was.

Tailored Solution: Versus "off-the-rack," this is a solution that is hand-crafted to a problem's specifics and peculiarities. And it's expensive.

Take Ownership: To take complete and personal responsibility for the success or failure of a project or task. Encouraged by management as a way to get employees to feel pride and commitment to their work, but it also means the employee will take the fall for a bomb.

Tangent: A line that goes off from a circle at a 90-degree angle. Or an idea that starts from the right place and then becomes a non sequitur.

Task Force: A team that is assigned to a specific objective with a limited time to achieve it. Task forces are like a hit squad, and are supposed to disband whether they succeed or fail, but they rarely do.

Team Player: On the one hand, you need to be an "energized," "empowered" "intrapreneur," taking "initiative" at every step as you complete the "mission." On the other hand, you earn all the real points by being a bureaucratic toady, sucking up to whatever you think senior management wants. It's really up to you.

Team: A group that's assigned a particular task or issue. Different from (no pretend time constraints) but similar to a task force.

Team Building: The assembling of groups of people with complementary skills and abilities for the purposes of attacking a project.

Team-oriented: Before a company can accomplish effective "team-building," it must decide it wants to work in teams, and then develop an action plan for team-building. This requires that everyone from the CEO on down get team-oriented.

Technoplegic: A person with the inability to properly use new technology.

Testability: The capacity for effective trial runs. And the ability to take a bunch of poking from colleagues without "going postal."

Test Chip: The prototypical computer chip used to determine the feasibility of producing more of the same chip in mass quantities. "Let's use the intern on this project as a test chip; if he gets it, we'll give him more."

Thin Client: An underperforming client. One whose value, in cash or repeat business terms, is disappointing.

Think Outside the Box: To problem-solve or create a concept or product using nontraditional approaches. Creators of the original Apple computer were known to think outside the box.

Thumbs-up: The big old go-ahead. Or the job-well-done signal. Or the phony I'm-with-ya nod. You pick.

Tight Integration: When projects, services, and people are well connected to the tools they're supposed to work with. Or not.

Time Frame: How long something will take. "What's your time frame on that, Bill?"

Time to Market: The time it takes from the inception of the original idea to the day the product is in the stores.

Timeline: How long is it gonna take? This does not simply refer to the time it takes to complete a project but also to all of the step deadlines in the middle. What's the timeline?

Top-down: When the top of the organization decides exactly what the bottom of the organization ought to be doing.

Touch Base: To contact. "I've been meaning to touch base with you about the Henderson account."

Touchy-Feelies: Unjustified, imprecisely accountable expenses and initiatives designed to make everybody feel good—or less bad. Self-congratulatory pizza lunches. Personal thank-yous for stuff the employee should be doing anyway just to collect his paycheck.

Tourists: People who take training classes just to get vacations from their jobs. "There were three serious students in the class; the rest were just tourists."

TQM: Total Quality Management. "Quality is free!" The theory is that the cost of fixing mistakes is way higher than the cost of avoiding the mistakes in the first place, and that processes that are designed to be error-free are more efficient. TQM is the science of designing for quality that exceeds customer requirements.

Train Wreck: The ugliest confluence of unfortunate events. There are usually few survivors. "The budget meeting was a train wreck. Edgar is probably gonna get fired for it."

Transcontinental Enterprise: To justify a claim of being a transcontinental enterprise, one must produce at least one invoice addressed to a foreign customer.

Transition: To move from one job or task or responsibility to another. This word used to be a noun but is now living large in verb land.

Truly Stackable: Describes a job or process or type of employee whose responsibilities and characteristics are so clear and defined and measurable that they can be perfectly and simply replicated, then stacked one on top of the other to save space for training time or recruitment costs.

Turnkey Operation: A system that is so streamlined and simplified, it can operate at the turn of a key in a door.

Turnkey Solution: The solution to a problem that is as easy as turning a key in the door or lifting the switch on a light. *See also* "turnkey operation."

Underperform: Disappoint entirely. Fail miserably. Generally suck.

Uninstalled: Fired. *See also* "decruitment."

Usage Report: The tabulation of transactions from the log file. How many people are doing it, whatever *it* is.

User-Friendly: Easy to use. Kindergarten simple.

User Scenario: Where you try to imagine what the pinhead at the user end of a product or service is going to do. "How do I plug this in?"

Value-added: Taken directly from the fast-food world of cheap, quick meals, "value-added" is a wonderful catchphrase that helps convince feeble-minded consumers that you're giving them more than they'd get anywhere else.

Value-adds: Features that make a product worth more than its obvious base value, to everyone involved.

Value Chain: Every contributing party along the path between the patch of dirt, the diamond in the rough, and the sparkler featured in Tiffany's window. Everyone who makes some germ of an idea grow into a product or service of value.

Value-focused: In the 1980s, business was profit-focused, but now, with the increased consumer care shown by companies,

companies are value-focused, concentrating on what they can offer their clients to keep them happy and smiling.

Value Preservation: The maintenance of a high level of worth throughout the duration of a project. No loss, all gain.

Vaporware: Software that was announced and promoted but never actually shipped. A big ta-da for a no-show.

Venture Capital: Money (someone else's) used to bankroll the start-ups with the hottest prospects.

Version Control: Otherwise known as "source control." Monitoring the creative process so you're not working like mad to revise what turns out to be an earlier, already discarded version of something. Wasted effort is pretty much what you're trying to avoid here.

Vertical Market: The specific market niches that truly need the product you're selling comprise the vertical market.

Virtual Organization: A company in which most of the work is done off-site, by free agents, and using all electronic means available. An excuse not to come into an office.

Vision: Being able to imagine realizing one's goals in the near or distant future. Often occurs while drinking heavily or while under the influence of an alternate hallucinogenic.

Visualization: When "dimensionalizing" an idea, you're engaged in visualizing a successful outcome. Picture it, babe.

Wasting Asset: Something you own that's going to be worth less tomorrow than it is today. A car is a wasting asset, and so is software code. On the other hand, real estate and market share have traditionally been growing assets.

Wear Different Hats: When one person plays a variety of roles within the same company.

Web Initiative: The effort of "newbies" tiptoeing their company into the digital future.

Web Presence: The amount of impact and visibility (or "footprint" or "real estate") a company has on the Internet.

Whatever It Takes: Immeasurable lengths. "I will do whatever it takes to make things right." Ha.

Whizzy: Cool, fast, slick, interesting, powerful, awesome, and neat.

Win-Win: Is it possible for someone to win without there being a loser? Sounds like a mutually beneficial relationship or situation where one is trying to balance a bunch of stuff to eliminate risk. Or punishment.

Window: The little opening that only the most highly trained, perfectly prepared competitor can identify and slip through—and success awaits on the other side. You can see a window in a meeting or in a market. If you see it, go for it.

Work Smarter: To work faster and more efficiently, and with fewer mistakes.

Work the Issue: To tamely and aimlessly mull over a problem, alone or in a group. What usually happens until the staff sergeant barks orders to get some resolve or get out.

Work-flow Management: The prescribed way work moves through an organization. Good work-flow management can dramatically decrease time and costs. Bad work-flow management can make you hemorrhage time and money.

Write Solid Code: To create computer code that's intelligent and relatively bug-free. It's pretty easy to write mediocre code, but the cost of fixing the inevitable bugs is higher than the cost of writing the code properly in the first place.

Xerox Subsidy: The worker's presumed right to help himself to the personal use of the office's copy equipment. *See also* "franking privileges."

Y2K: Short for "Year 2000," that apocalyptic point on the horizon that, besides simply marking the new millennium, marks the pending doom for shortsighted, dimwitted (that is to say, almost all) computers and software created before 1997. Can't wait!

Year 2000: During the Cold War, programmers must have figured the world would end or their computers would be replaced by the year 2000, so they didn't bother to program the computers to properly deal with the recording of time into a new century. The good news is that virtually all profit hits, software failures, or customer service screw-ups can be blamed on this bug. *See also* "Y2K."

Year 2000 Compliant: If every time you write a date you include four extra digits, then you won't stop working, shut down, or die when we hit the next century. Plus, you'll be year 2000 compliant.

Year-ends: The end-of-the-year reports on all things business, from sales to cash flow to productivity. Year-ends are both legitimate measurement tools and annual report cards and they pretty much indicate whether a manager (and those she manages) can expect a bonus or should start reading the want ads.

Zero Bug Count: Not perfect, bug-free software, as you would imagine, but software with the major, "actionable" bugs removed.

Zero Sum Game: A negotiation in which there's a fixed amount to go around, and what I don't win, you get. Opposite of "win-win."

The Buzzword Bingo Game Cards

**Fifty Clip 'n' Save Buzzword Bingo Cards
to use at work, at home, at school!**

The Buzzword Bingo Game Card

Interactive Feedback	Facilitate	Think Outside the Box	Corporate Image	1:1
Value-added	Massively Parallel	Flatten	Off-site	Low-Hanging Fruit
Critical Success Factor	Force Management	FREE	Locked and Loaded	Experience Curve
Smell Test	Reality Check	Dynamic Network	Vertical Market	Gold-Star
Bandwidth	Proactive	Partner (verb)	Micro-manage	Web Presence

The **Buzzword Bingo** Game Card

Across the Organization	Goal Congruence	Work-flow Management	Downsizing	Blamestorming
Scope the Creep	Network	Dialogue	Dynamic Network	Xerox Subsidy
Operationalize	Annotation	FREE	Hollywired	Content
Fault Tolerance	Go Forward	Out of the Loop	Win-Win	Global Strategy
Closure	Drive	Productize	Incent	Marketplace Scenarios

The **Buzzword Bingo** Game Card

End User	Stretch Goal	Branding	Homogeneous System	Paperless Office
Share of Market	Implement	Year 2000 Compliant	Action Item	Reorg
Train Wreck	Smartsize	FREE	Encapsulate	F2F
Vision	Pass the Baton	Regression Test	Value Preservation	Globalization
Bug	Beta Release	Chainsaw Consultant	Mentor	Franking Privileges

The **Buzzword Bingo** Game Card

Siliwood	Quality Gaps	Bullet	Cube Farm	Organic Growth
Alpha Release	Media-rich	Underperform	Whizzy	Downsize
Emotional Economics	Constituencies	FREE	Litmus Test	Cost-Reduction Strategies
Betamaxed	Socialize the Idea	Dancing Baloney	Going Forward	Spin-off
Barrier to Entry	Real Estate	Business Silo	Mission	Site-based

The **Buzzword Bingo** Game Card

Team Player	Web Initiative	Context	Get Your Input	Betamaxed
Stretch Goal	Productize	Experience Curve	Scalable Technologies	Comfort Zone
Release	Fixed in the Next Release	**FREE**	Multitasker	Admin Tools
Generica	Soup to Nuts	Write Solid Code	Blamestorming	Functionality Freeze
Smoke Text	Champion	FTP (verb)	Asynchronous	Vaporware

The **Buzzword Bingo** Game Card

Postmortem	Legacy	Cash-intensive	Productize	Out of Pocket
High Dome	Issues	Enabler	Infrastructure	24/7
Flesh Out	Spin-off	FREE	Closure	Anchoring Concept
Go-to-Market Strategy	Cost-effective	Query	Cost Management	Ineffectual
Encapsulate	Best in Class	Guesstimate	Pass the Baton	Scalable Technologies

The **Buzzword Bingo** Game Card

Passion	Get One's Ducks in a Row	Fungible	User Scenarios	Partner (noun)
Increased Communication	Drive	Tight Integration	Economies of Scale	Knowledge Management
Org Chart	Gatekeeper	FREE	Web Initiative	Take Ownership
Cash Cow	Outsource	Force Management	Infuse	Connectivity
RL	Disintermediation	Groupware	Network	Roll-up

The **Buzzword Bingo** Game Card

Available for Reassignment	Smoke Test	Value-focused	Incubate	Mutually Beneficial
Create a New Space	Timeline	Pass the Baton	Cobweb	Go-to-Market Strategy
Portal	On Board	FREE	Value Preservation	ALARA
Going Forward	Customer Retention	Motivation	Rapid Deployment	Encapsulate
Marketplace Scenarios	Franking Privileges	Barrier to Entry	Cost Management	RL

The **Buzzword Bingo** Game Card

Cash-intensive	Portal	Stratical	Skill Set	Rightsize
Alliance	Rathole	Functionality Freeze	Strategic Planning	Asynchronous
FTP (verb)	Work the Issue	FREE	Ambiguous Navigation	BPR
Heterogeneous System	Spin-off	Big Win	More Bang for the Buck	Release
Flexible Technology	Co-create	Institutional Rigidity	High Dome	Partner (verb)

The **Buzzword Bingo** Game Card

Exit Strategy	Facetime	Network	FREE	Processes	Red Flag
Ground-Level Action	Heritage	Market-driven		Co-opetition	Did You Run Purify?
Aggregate	Fungible	FREE		Usage Report	Soup to Nuts
Hollywired	Step Up to It	Leverage		Fixed in the Next Release	Perot
Infrastructure	Shared Space	Energized		Create a New Space	Revector

The **Buzzword Bingo** Game Card

Fixed in the Next Release	Ramp Up	Bug	Structural Constraints	Cost Management
Mutually Beneficial	Disintermediation	Ambiguous Navigation	Net Out	Y2K
Stretch Goal	Cognitive Development	FREE	Boutique-style	Increased Communication
Synergy	Productize	Content	On the Cutting Edge	Gating Factor
Work Smarter	Self-Fulfilling Prophecy	Best of Breed	Challenges	Bullet

The **Buzzword Bingo** Game Card

Mutually Beneficial	Dimensionalize	Microplug-in	Future Gazing	Reality Check
Closure	Implement	Cube Farm	Mission-Critical	Share of Wallet
Motivation	Window	FREE	Enabler	Speak to an Issue
Design Considerations	Usage Report	Team	Push Authority Down the Pyramid	Pass the Baton
Cost-Reduction Strategies	Flexible	Lay-down	Available for Reassignment	Create a New Space

The **Buzzword Bingo** Game Card

Revolutionary	Value-added	Skill Set	Chainsaw Consultant	Raise the Bar
Smartsize	Facetime	Opportunity	Desensification	Softball
Declining Core Technology	Testability	FREE	Drop-Dead Date	Usage Report
Business Silo	Cross-Matrix	Bug	Ground-level Action	User Scenario
Visualization	Real Time	Gating Factor	Cube Farm	Interoperable

The **Buzzword Bingo** Game Card

Algorithm	Future Gazing	Action Item	Reciprocity	Business Casual
Win-Win	Visualization	Cube Farm	Value Preservation	Go Live
Learning Curve	Media-rich	FREE	Year 2000	Emotional Economics
Tailored Solution	Protocol	On Board	Gating Factor	Geographically Dispersed
Boutique-style	GUI	Top-down	TQM	Globalization

The **Buzzword Bingo** Game Card

Query	Ad-hoc	Turnkey Operation	Operationalize	Blamestorming
FTP (verb)	Permission	Go Forward	Dynamic Network	Network
Context	Value Preservation	FREE	Test Chip	Net-Net
Take Ownership	Quantify	Analysis Paralysis	Chainsaw Consultant	Enabler
Declining Core Technology	Ball's in Your Court	Re-engineer	BPR	Fungible

The **Buzzword Bingo** Game Card

Asset	Enabler	Brain Dump	More Bang for the Buck	Encapsulate
Facilitators	Facilitate	Postmodern	Analysis Paralysis	Going Forward
Critical Path	Business Casual	FREE	Touch Base	Write Solid Code
Franking Privileges	Scope Creep	Step Up to It	ALARA	Action Item
Get Your Input	Partner (noun)	Test Chip	Ad-hoc	User Friendly

The **Buzzword Bingo** Game Card

Newbie	Content	Think Outside the Box	Backload	Tangent
Business Model	Regression Test	Zero Sum Game	Touch Base	Design Considerations
Barrier to Entry	Boutique-style	FREE	Cash-intensive	Mutually Beneficial
Revector	Big Picture	Cash Cow	Signage	Objective
Re-engineer	Cube Farm	Value Chain	Decruitment	Aggregate

The **Buzzword Bingo** Game Card

Blamestorming	Incent	Coaches	Ball's in Your Court	Go Live
Operationalize	Turnkey Solution	Funnel it Down	Ineffectual	Best of Breed
Speak to an Issue	Flesh Out	FREE	Version Control	Strategic Planning
Going Postal	Hollywired	Breakout Session	Sweet Spot	Geographically Dispersed
Share of Wallet	Scripting	Reorg	Mission-critical	Transition

The **Buzzword Bingo** Game Card

Wear Different Hats	Big Picture	Mission	Org Chart	Value-added
Constituencies	Effectual	Downsizing	Best Thinking	Opt In
Energized	Legacy	FREE	Tourists	Deployment
Idea Hamsters	Socialize the Idea	Xerox Subsidy	Go Live	Mutually Beneficial
Cross-Platform Technology	Passion	Paperless Office	Year-ends	Mentor

The **Buzzword Bingo** Game Card

Goal-oriented	Cross-Matrix	Deployment	Tangent	Attack the Problem
Zero Bug Count	Senior Management	Uninstalled	Betamaxed	Team Player
Design Reusability	Big Picture	FREE	Thumbs-up	High Dome
Bandwidth	Barrier to Entry	PEBCAK	Y2K	Connectivity
Bullet	Close the Loop	Actualize	Off-site	Media-rich

The **Buzzword Bingo** Game Card

Fungible	Enabler	Force Management	Franking Privileges	Partner (verb)
Exit Strategy	Cash Cow	Proof-of-Concept	Killer Apps	Blamestorming
Cost-effective	Challenges	FREE	Revector	Make It Happen
Socialize the Idea	Mission from God	Neophyte	Benefit	Have a Lot on One's Plate
Geographically Dispersed	Integration	Future Gazing	Heterogeneous System	Interactive Feedback

The **Buzzword Bingo** Game Card

Percussive Maintenance	Intellectual Property	Site-based	Ineffectual	Opt In
Smell Test	Mission-critical	Productize	1:1	Decruitment
Zero Bug Count	Flexible	FREE	Legacy	Perot
Outsource	Value-focused	Going Forward	Media-rich	Disincent
Issues	Design Reusability	Disconnect	Business Casual	Co-create

The Buzzword Bingo Game Card

Marketplace Scenarios	Content Provider	Re-engineer	Micro-manage	Revolutionary
Critical Path	Co-create	Pilot Error	Ping	Information Deficit
Intellectual Property	Ramp Up	FREE	Desensification	Breakout Session
Productize	Boutique-style	1:1	Open-Door Policy	Global Strategy
Locked and Loaded	Seamless	Ego Surfing	Get Your Input	Newbie

The **Buzzword Bingo** Game Card

Value-added	Economics of Scale	Scalable Technologies	Whatever It Takes	Band-Aid
Dancing Baloney	Usage Report	Dialogue	Entrenched	Mentor
Bullet	Proprietary	FREE	Thin Client	Go-date
Signage	Go Live	Flatten	Deep Weeds	Obligating Question
Flexible	Mutually Beneficial	Source Control	Get a Handle On	Institutional Rigidity

The **Buzzword Bingo** Game Card

Going Forward	Get a Handle On	Global Strategy	Design Considerations	Enabling Technology
Blamestorming	Admin Tools	Alliance	Middleware	Siliwood
GUI	Technoplegic	FREE	24/7	Self-Manage
Step Up to It	Ramp Up	Extract	Quantify	Transition
404	Franking Privileges	Work Smarter	Hyperarchy	Marketplace Scenarios

The **Buzzword Bingo** Game Card

Legacy	Dialogue	Y2K	Going Forward	Sweating Your Assets
Put the Genie Back in the Bottle	Senior Management	Shared Space	Massively Parallel	Open-Door Policy
Increased Communication	Year 2000	FREE	Beepilepsy	Admin Tools
Brain Dump	Dimensionalize	Prairie Dogging	Dynamic Network	Entrenched
Business Casual	Value-focused	Bleeding Edge	Emotional Economics	Percussive Maintenance

The **Buzzword Bingo** Game Card

Media-rich	Drive	Smoke Test	Marketplace Scenarios	Cognitive Development
Groupware	Desensification	Bug	Operational Excellence	Work the Issue
Ground-Level Action	Cost Management	FREE	Functionality	Multitasker
Synthesis	Scripting	Time to Market	Ego Surfing	Guesstimate
Resource-constrained	Co-opetition	Turnkey Solution	Best Practices	Leverage

The **Buzzword Bingo** Game Card

Did You Run Purify?	Smell Test	Seamless	Skill Set	Incubate
Start-up Artist	Coaches	Create a New Space	Streamline	Analysis Paralysis
Common Platform	FC Release	FREE	Forecast	Percussive Maintenance
Franking Privileges	Backload	Context	F2F	Sweating Your Assets
Win-Win	Discrete	Mind Share	Net Out	Thumbs-up

The **Buzzword Bingo** Game Card

Interactive	Testability	Algorithm	Y2K	Cherry Picking
Smoke Test	Cash Cow	Core Competency	Pilot Error	Mentor
Truly Stackable	Raise the Bar	FREE	Push Authority Down the Pyramid	Train Wreck
Media-rich	Close the Loop	Interface	Functionality Freeze	Stratical
Design Considerations	Buy In	Year 2000 Compliant	Big Win	Funnel It Down

The **Buzzword Bingo** Game Card

IMHO	Litmus Test	Barrier to Entry	Mission Statement	Interactive Feedback
Turnkey Solution	Infrastructure	Multitasker	Self-Fulfilling Prophecy	Force Management
Roll Out a Server	Impactful	FREE	Fixed in the Next Release	Beepilepsy
Year 2000 Compliant	Assmosis	Enabling Technology	Tight Integration	Benefit
Functionality Freeze	End User	Think Outside the Box	High Dome	Resource-constrained

The **Buzzword** Bingo Game Card

Best in Class	Dancing Baloney	Proposition	Tangent	Annotate
Write Solid Code	Paradigm	Just in Time	At IBM/Microsoft/Stanford/MIT We...	Signage
Chainsaw Consultant	Heritage	FREE	No-brainer	Drag and Drop
Reciprocity	Red Flag	Cognitive Development	Org Chart	Smell Test
Buy In	FTP (verb)	Window	Uninstalled	Web Initiative

The **Buzzword Bingo** Game Card

Drag and Drop	Get One's Ducks in a Row	Operationalize	Infuse	Locked and Loaded
Wasting Asset	Geographically Dispersed	Work-flow Management	Visualization	Get a Handle On
Step Up to It	Business Casual	FREE	Level Playing Field	Idea Hamsters
User Scenarios	Turnkey Solution	Platform Agnostic	Best Thinking	Hollywired
Partner (noun)	Declining Core Technology	Affiliate Program	Extranet	Obligating Question

The **Buzzword Bingo** Game Card

Decruitment	Information Deficit	Reality Check	Visualization	Timeline
Lay-down	Quarterlies	Revenue-generating	90% Solution	Coaches
Signage	Collectively as a Group	FREE	Cash Cow	Branding
Price Point	GUI	No-brainer	Going Forward	Shared Space
Transcontinental Enterprise	Metrics	Generica	Shake the Dead Leaves Out of the Trees	Team-oriented

The **Buzzword Bingo** Game Card

Postmortem	Intellectual Property	Incubate	Milestone	Effectual
Beepilepsy	Idea Hamsters	Facilitators	Impactful	Gating Factor
Soup to Nuts	Integration	FREE	Partner (noun)	Synthesis
Share of Wallet	Paperless Office	Strategic Planning	Risk Management	Year-ends
TQM	Initiative	Decruitment	Real Estate	Scope

The **Buzzword Bingo** Game Card

Extract	Customer Intimacy	Intranet	Incent	Go Forward
Quality Gaps	Download	Release	Team Player	Organic Growth
Come on Board	Internet	FREE	Alliance	Microplug-in
Fungible	Self-paced	Infuse	Off-site	On Board
Flesh Out	Comfort Zone	Analysis Paralysis	Transcontinental Enterprise	Roll-up

The **Buzzword Bingo** Game Card

Underperform	Mentor	Bullet	Multitasker	Continuous Improvement
Testability	Band-Aid	Corporate Image	Proof-of-Concept	Encapsulate
Venture	Ball's in Your Court	FREE	Design Considerations	Ramp Up
Future Gazing	Release	Barrier to Entry	Make It Happen	Corporate Culture
Timeline	Bandwidth	Interface	Ideate	Take Ownership

The **Buzzword Bingo** Game Card

Perot	Mission Statement	Champion	Vision	Reference (verb)
Affiliate Program	Partner (noun)	End User	Paperless Office	Challenges
Value Preservation	Soup to Nuts	FREE	Cube Farm	Ego Surfing
Skill Set	Operationalize	Facilitators	Smell Test	Beta Release
Query	Think Outside the Box	In the Know	Alliance	Ping

The **Buzzword Bingo** Game Card

Permission	Structural Constraints	Passion	Partner (verb)	Site-based
Internet	End User	Backload	Franking Privileges	State-of-the-Art
Download	Network	FREE	Proprietary	Mouse Milking
Revector	Management Style	Interactive Feedback	Cost-Reduction Strategies	Open-Door Policy
Alliance	Web Presence	Deliverable	Block Scheduling	Break the Rules

The **Buzzword Bingo** Game Card

Big Picture	Enabler	Marketplace Scenarios	Net-Net	Admin Tools
Disconnect	Signage	Attack the Problem	Productize	Barrier to Entry
On the Cutting Edge	ALARA	FREE	Core Competency	Break the Rules
Co-opt	Nonsequenced Instruction	Dialogue	Experience Curve	Transcontinental Enterprise
Forecast	TQM	Organizational Information Base	Business Silo	Beepilepsy

The **Buzzword Bingo** Game Card

Version Control	Roll-up	Institutional Rigidity	Force Management	Benchmark
Across the Organization	PEBCAK	Assmosis	Exit Strategy	Integration
RL	Excellence	FREE	Business Model	F2F
Common Platform	Share of Market	Content	On the Cutting Edge	Declining Core Technology
Network	24/7	In the Know	Affiliate Program	Blamestorming

The **Buzzword Bingo** Game Card

Best Practices	Brain Dump	Work Smarter	Middleware	Aggregate
Seamless	Take Ownership	Knowledge Management	Shake the Dead Leaves Out of the Trees	Issues
Milestone	Version Control	FREE	IMHO	Business Model
Intranet	Implement	Team-oriented	Socialize the Idea	Quality Gaps
Initiative	Year 2000	Structural Constraints	Feedback	Desensification

The Buzzword Bingo Game Card

Smoke Test	Litmus Test	Cost-Reduction Strategies	Quality Gaps	Extract
Enabling Technology	Version Control	Comfort Zone	Truly Stackable	Reference (verb)
Heritage	Go-to-Market Strategy	FREE	Disintermediation	User Scenarios
On the Cutting Edge	Make It Happen	Roll-up	F2F	Co-create
Whatever It Takes	Customer Intimacy	Start-up Artist	Cross-Matrix	On Board

The **Buzzword Bingo** Game Card

Multitasker	Action Item	Technoplegic	Opportunity	Media-rich
Neophyte	Window	Siliwood	Idea Hamsters	Global Strategy
Constituencies	Processes	FREE	Uninstalled	Touch Base
Business Model	Market-driven	Flesh Out	Paperless Office	Flexible Technology
Milestone	Opt In	Value-adds	Anchoring Concept	Suite of Tools

The **Buzzword Bingo** Game Card

Visualization	Revector	RL	Enabler	Net-Net
Site-based	Geographically Dispersed	Market-driven	Asynchronous	Operationalize
Experience Curve	Self Fulfilling Prophecy	FREE	BPR	Keyboard Plaque
Heritage	Come on Board	Facilitate	Siliwood	Cognitive Development
Vertical Market	At IBM/Microsoft/Stanford/MIT we...	Annotate	Best Thinking	Across the Organization

The **Buzzword Bingo** Game Card

Enabler	Corporate Culture	Brain Dump	Mutually Beneficial	Stratical
Flesh Out	FC Release	Essential Drivers	Increased Communication	Make It Happen
Web Presence	Re-engineer	FREE	Fault Tolerance	Deep Weeds
Out of the Loop	Hyperarchy	Business Silo	Decruitmant	Ad hoc
Intranet	Connectivity	Major Players	Train Wreck	Outsource

The Alternative Buzzword Bingo Game Cards

Sports! Politics! Awards show! Education! Every category of
life has its own set of buzzwords. So Buzzword Bingo can
be played wherever you are, whatever you're doing.
Watching an ESPN sports roundup? Whip out your sports
Buzzword Bingo card and see how quickly you can yell
"Bingo!" Try these alternative cards on for size, or use our
blank cards to make up your own.

The Buzzword Bingo Game Card—Sports

Big Game	Going All the Way	Dinger	Texas Leaguer	Clubhouse Leader
Lotta Heart	Nickel Package	Do It for the Gipper	Doing the Dance	Can't Pull the Trigger
Calling the Bullpen	Wicked Slice	FREE	Knock It In the Jar	Frozen Rope
Sixth Man	Pay Dirt	Triple Threat	Fine Young Man	Came to Play
Showboat	Throw Heat	Golf Shot	Take Them Deep	True Competitor

The **Buzzword Bingo** Game Card—**Washington Politics**

Impact (verb)	Nanny Problem	Photo Op	Pork!	Military Strongman
Gutter Politics	Foggy Bottom	Inside the Beltway	High-Ranking White House Official	Gucci Gulch Lobbyist
Ground Swell of Support	High Negatives	FREE	On the Stump	Rubber Chicken Circuit
Smoking Gun	The Hill	Play the Race Card	Do It for the Gipper	Policy Wonk
FOB	Bellweather State	1600 Pennsylvania Avenue	Intern Problem	Grassroots Campaign

The Buzzword Bingo Game Card—Awards Show

Members of the Academy	Fellow Nominees	I Had a Speech Prepared	Mom	Good Roles for Women
God	Really Like Me	King of the World	Director	Agent
Hanks	This Thing Is Really Heavy	FREE	Surprised	Vision
Believed in Me	Refugees	Without Whom	Script	Speechless
I Don't Know What to Say!	Spielberg	Creator	I'm Sure I Left Someone Out	Do It for the Gipper

The Buzzword Bingo Game Card—Education

Team Leader	Learning Styles	Site-Based Team	Solution	Project Approach
Concerned Parent	Outcome-Based	Curriculum	Expertise	Mainstreamed
Assessment Piece	Special Needs	FREE	Integrated Curriculum	Emotionalize
Diversity	Partnership	Student-centered	Enriched Learning	Authentic Assessment
Co-Teach	Fun	Educationally Sound	Thematic Units	Under-funded

The **Buzzword Bingo** Game Card

		FREE		

The **Buzzword Bingo** Game Card

FREE

About the Authors

LARA STEIN is president of iXL-New York, the interactive multimedia agency, and was ranked one of *The Silicon Alley Reporter*'s Top 100 executives. Lara has also worked with MSN's Microsoft Multimedia Productions (M3P), Marvel Comics, and Lifetime TV. She lives in New York.

BENJAMIN YOSKOVITZ is a co-founder and vice president of sales and marketing for meep!media, inc., a firm specializing in Web and intranet development. He lives in Montreal.

Visit the Buzzword Bingo Web site at www.buzzwordbingo.com.